WHO'S HOLDING YOUR LADDER?

Copyright © 2025 by Sam Chand

Published by AVAIL

All rights reserved. No portion of this book may be reproduced, stored in a retrieval system, or transmitted in any form or by any means—electronic, mechanical, photocopy, recording, scanning, or other—except for brief quotations in critical reviews or articles, without prior written permission of the author.

Unless otherwise specified, all Scripture quotations are taken from the King James Version of the Bible. Public domain. | Scripture quotations marked AMP are taken from the Amplified® Bible (AMP), Copyright © 2015 by The Lockman Foundation. Used by permission. www.lockman.org | Scripture quotations marked NKJV are taken from the New King James Version®. Copyright © 1982 by Thomas Nelson. Used by permission. All rights reserved.

For foreign and subsidiary rights, contact the author.

Cover design by: Sara Young
Cover photo by: Andrew van Tilborgh

ISBN: 978-1-964794-72-3   1 2 3 4 5 6 7 8 9 10

Printed in the United States of America

WHO'S HOLDING YOUR LADDER?

SELECTING YOUR LEADERS
Leadership's Most Critical Decision

SAM CHAND

CONTENTS

CHAPTER 1. Who's Holding Your Ladder?. 9

CHAPTER 2. What Kind of Person Is Holding Your Ladder?. 27

CHAPTER 3. Five Core Qualities of Ladder Holders . . 39

CHAPTER 4. How Do We Recruit Volunteers? 63

CHAPTER 5. Are We Managing Ladders?. 81

CHAPTER 6. Can We Turn Ladder Holders into Ladder Climbers?. 105

CHAPTER 7. Are We Looking Up the Ladder? 127

CHAPTER 8. How Did Jesus Choose Ladder Holders? 135

CHAPTER 9. Whose Ladder Are You Holding?. 141

Teaching This Material 151

Endnotes 159

1
WHO'S HOLDING YOUR LADDER?

I stared out the window while I waited for someone to call me into the sanctuary. I was a featured speaker at a conference at Evangel Church in Queens, New York. As I meditated on the points I wanted to cover, something in the street below diverted my attention.

A man stood on a ladder painting—not a terribly uncommon sight. I smiled, remembering my student days in Bible college. I had spent my summers doing that kind of work. Yet I couldn't take my eyes off the man. For several minutes I watched his graceful motions as he moved his brush across the surface.

"I wonder who's holding the ladder for him?" I asked aloud. I couldn't see all the way to the street level.

As I stood in pastor Robert Johansson's study, I kept thinking of that question. Someone had to be down there bracing the painter's ladder although I couldn't see him. My impression was made while I stared down from about eight floors above street level. As I watched the man paint the exterior wall, I noticed he could cover only a limited area. He stretched as far as he could to the left and right, reaching above his head. As I observed him, it occurred to me that he only climbed and reached the height in which he was comfortable.

> Whether in management or systems, the effectiveness of a leader depends on the person or persons who hold the ladder; those who are in support roles.

What would allow him to go higher? I asked myself. I could see that he stood on an extension ladder so he could go higher—and he would have to if he wanted to finish the job. If the ladder reached the top of the building, he still needed one thing. He needed someone on the street level to hold his ladder steady while he worked.

By himself, the painter couldn't go any farther. He had stretched and reached and done everything he could by himself. He needed help.

As I watched his graceful strokes, I thought about that action in leadership terms. It struck me that, whether in management or systems, a leader's effectiveness depends on the person or persons who hold the ladder—those in support roles.

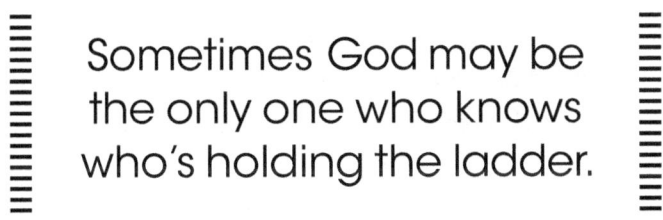

Sometimes God may be the only one who knows who's holding the ladder.

Then another thought struck me: Those who hold the ladders are as important as the leaders themselves. My mind wouldn't let go of that image. As I stared out that window in Queens, I kept thinking, no leader gets to the top without those who hold the ladder below. I craned my neck trying to see the street level, but I never could see who held that ladder.

Then I smiled as my mind shifted to the symbolism of leadership, success, and people in enabling roles. Those who fully support the bottom are often unseen. That doesn't diminish their importance or the need for them, but it does mean that even though their ministries or their positions are every bit as important as the painter on the top, sometimes they do their work unnoticed. Sometimes God may be the only one who knows who's holding the ladder.

I took the idea even further. I began to think of the ladder as the symbol of the dream—the vision of the leader—and, of course, that makes the painter the visionary. Once the visionaries start up their ladders, ministry can be large and far-reaching, or narrow and confined. The visionaries could have all the training possible, the most expensive equipment, years of experience and knowledge about painting, and all the expertise with extreme passionate for what they do, but none of these is the deciding factor in how high the visionary can climb. It is the ladder holder who determines the height of the ladder climber. "That's it!" I cried out. "Those who hold the ladder control the ascent of the visionaries."

> The ladder holder determines the height of the ladder climber. Those who hold the ladder control the ascent of the visionaries.

LADDERS AND LEADERSHIP

Long after I left the conference in Queens, I continued to dwell on that idea. I considered how that concept applies to leadership in business or in the church. Immediately, I remembered three examples (or paradigms as we like to call them today). I first heard them delivered as part of a powerful message by pastor Gerald Brooks from Grace Outreach Center in Plano, Texas. In a large conference I attended, he pointed out that there are three ways in which we do ministry.

The first is to do everything ourselves. That's how a number of leaders try to function, especially when the congregation is small. Eventually the realization hits: *That's too much work.*

The second is to hire it out. Some churches pay others to take over part or all of the load. *That's too much money.*

The third is to develop others. Some leaders teach people how to do the tasks. *That's too much time.*

> **There are three ways in which we do ministry:**
> *The first* is to do everything ourselves. That's too much work.
> *The second* is to hire it out. That's too much money.
> *The third* one is to develop others. That's too much time.

Pastor Brooks pointed out that he had given us three paradigms and all of them had drawbacks. "What is the wise thing to do?" he asked.

> **There is a vast difference between training people and developing them. Training focuses on tasks; developing focuses on the person.**

Obviously, the answer is the third option—to develop others. However, too many church leaders get so busy painting at the top of their own ladders, they don't realize how much help they need. They don't realize the importance of developing ladder holders until they're sixty feet above ground looking down. Because they didn't teach others to hold the ladders for them, a few visionaries have fallen. Others have burned out from overwork, trying to do everything themselves. Some have simply quit trying. "It's just too hard," they say, "and too lonely." If they had only known there was a simple (though not easy) way to climb higher, perhaps they would still be going strong today. Therein lies the irony of it all—they quit because of something that appears too hard as they take the hardest possible route.

I have carefully chosen the term *developing* others because it is unique from training—there is a vast difference between the two. Training focuses on tasks; developing focuses on the person. Training is uni-directional; developing is omni-directional. We train people to become receptionists. When we're finished, they're good receptionists and they do their tasks well, but we have not developed them so that they are ready to move into other positions.

God never intended for the local church to be a one-person organization. That takes us back to the concept of developing leaders. If we don't develop and equip others, we're never going to have the kind of ladder holders we need—especially when we want to climb to the highest rungs.

> We leaders need ladder holders the most when we make the jump from activities to working with individuals.

Perhaps the best way to show how this works is to consider the contrast between *projects* and *people*. We leaders need ladder holders the most when we make the jump from activities to working with individuals. Projects involve policies, programs, buildings, ideas, or systems. Those are fairly stable and easily understood. We can usually control the variables. When we move beyond projects, not only have we made a major leap, but we also have to change our way of thinking. We can't treat people the way we treat ideas or activities. Obviously, most people are egocentric and more concerned about themselves than with others. That is, they don't naturally care about serving God or others. That's something they have to learn in their growth process. Realizing that fact about human nature forces us to constantly tailor the way we develop others, adapting to their ever-evolving tendencies, ways of thinking, and growth patterns. We need to help those we develop to

> » understand their purpose,
> » grasp why their roles are important,
> » cope with disappointment as well as with success,
> » ignite their passion
> » be inspired to reach their fullest potential.

Some leaders feel as if they're progressing simply because they are active. They point to the commotion and noise level around them. In reality, they may be going backward. Having many activities and projects doesn't always translate to advancement. The proof comes when the tumult ceases. That's when people realize that "action" has been taking them backward because a harsh reality hits them—not much has really changed. All of the noise, busyness, and hustle and bustle were really just a smokescreen for productivity.

We lead people, but we manage things.

This happens when leaders move from projects to people. Because they're not set up or taught to deal with people, they take the road less traveled and go back to where they are comfortable—projects. That is, they end up managing rather than leading. We lead *people*, but we manage *things*.

Sometimes trying to move from projects to people ends in messy scandals, deep-seated anger, and serious recriminations. Many things are happening—even good things—but they don't extend the kingdom of God or enable Christians to grow.

Too many of those who call themselves leaders are actually just good at projects. They can visualize what needs to be done. They are aware that unless the waters miraculously part, they'll need to build a bridge to take them across the Jordan River. They're often conscious of the need to get to the other side of the river while everyone else is enjoying the water. They grasp the problems involved in making a structure strong enough or wide enough. Those are not bad qualities—in fact, they are needed—but they are insufficient. Too often, they don't know how to get those tasks done because they don't know how to work well with people. They're aware only that they need a bridge built, and they can't understand why everyone doesn't volunteer and pitch in to accomplish the task. *They are project leaders.*

If they don't have excellent people skills, they focus on managing others—assigning jobs to people just to get the task completed. They have little concern for the talents or interests of those who are doing the task. "Just get it done," is the first sentence in their vocabulary.

This shows a crucial difference in leadership.

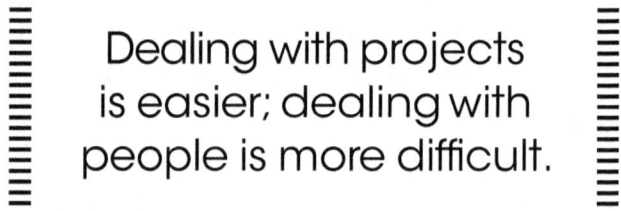

Project leaders see the need, and we admire their concern to get things finished. They're not very concerned about who does what, so long as they get the bridge built and the ark of the covenant and all the priestly equipment carried safely across the Jordan.

In short, dealing with projects is easier; dealing with people is more difficult. But you can't have one without the other. They are in a dependent relationship with one another.

By the time the project leaders set up camp on the east side of the Jordan, someone begins to realize that doing projects and building bridges aren't what really counts. They need bridges, of course, but they realize that the priorities are wrong. In the end, God's kingdom matures and stretches through people being edified, appreciated, and developed. In God's eyes, people count more than bridges, elevators, escalators, or ladders. All projects need people—but they need the right kind. They especially need the committed, talented workers to build the bridge correctly.

> In God's eyes, people count more than bridges, elevators, escalators, or ladders.

THE RIGHT LADDER HOLDERS

For days after I left Pastor Johansson's church, I thought about the ladder holders. I've been around thousands of leaders both in the marketplace and in ministry. I've come to one foundational understanding: The most important decision leaders make—whether it's to build a bridge across the Jordan or erect ladders to scale the walls of enemy strongholds—is to select the right helpers. If they don't have the right people holding the ladder, the project will fail.

In the church, we need to choose leaders who are involved, active, and already showing their commitment to Jesus Christ by their involvement. In business, we need the same kind of dedication. When we look at the qualities we seek, however, before anything else, we need to start with integrity.

> The most important decision leaders make is to select the right helpers.

Does that sound obvious? It may not be. I have a friend who became pastor of a church where they had a board of fifteen elders. Annually, the congregation elected five elders who served three years. That sounded fine, but the problem my friend faced was the election of those five elders each year.

He felt frustrated because most of the elders didn't attend Sunday school and yet they made decisions about the educational programs. Several of them didn't tithe, and yet they were the people who made decisions about church finances. Three of them attended church about once a month and spent more Sundays on the golf course than at worship, and yet they made the decisions about evangelism and outreach.

"Why did you elect him?" the pastor asked about one elder.

"To honor him. He's been in this church all his life and his daddy was an elder."

"He is one of the best businessmen in the city and people respect his decisions," said another. "He can help us make good decisions."

"If we make him an elder," was another response, "maybe he'll become an active leader."

"Make him an active leader," my friend countered, "and then make him an elder."

> Ultimately, the fulfillment of the vision depends on the people who support the ladder of the visionary leader.

The church continued to elect uncommitted elders for two more years before my pastor friend could get the congregation to understand the need for integrity. It took another two years before he had a church board that functioned with vision and commitment. By the end of the fifth year of his ministry, he had people in leadership who faithfully worshiped every week and gave at least ten percent of their income. Some taught Sunday school, sang in the choir, or participated in study groups. All of them had proven themselves in some form of ministry *before* they became elders. In short, they were people of integrity.

Why is this quality so crucial? The answer is that ultimately, the fulfillment of the vision depends on the people who support the ladder of the visionary leader.

Here's an example of how this works. I can change the light bulb in the ceiling in my living room. That's not a big problem because all I need is a six-foot stepladder. I can stand on whatever rung I need to reach the fixture. I don't need anyone to hold my ladder. What happens if the bulbs on the outside that illuminate my driveway need changing (they are two stories up from the ground)? I can't change them from inside the house or by leaning down from the roof. The only way to change the bulbs is to use a twenty-foot ladder.

To stand twenty feet above the ground on a piece of wood eighteen by six inches is scary enough. What happens if the ladder begins to sway? What happens if I get up there and reach just an inch too far to the left? I need someone to hold my ladder.

A situation like that actually happened to me. One evening we had invited friends over to celebrate the birthday of our daughter, Rachel. She had turned eighteen. My wife Brenda had worked hard getting the house ready for guests. Earlier in the week she had given me a few outdoor chores to do, and one of them was to change the floodlights. I had forgotten to do that task.

Fifteen minutes before our first guests were due, I went to snap on the outside lights, and they didn't come on. Then I remembered: I had forgotten to put in a new bulb.

"I'll get it done," I yelled as I raced into the garage, grabbed a bulb, and pulled out my handy dandy, fold-up Home Depot ladder. I set it up next to the garage. Then I turned around and looked at the distance from the ground. Until that moment, I hadn't realized how high the light was from the ground. I was experienced in climbing up and down ladders, so I shrugged. Just one bulb—no big deal. I started climbing. About two-thirds of the way up, I felt the ladder begin to wobble—just a little—but enough that I knew it wasn't safe to keep going.

"Rachel! Come and help," I called. "I need you to hold the ladder for me."

My daughter came outside and stared at me, not sure what she was supposed to do. She leaned forward with an arm on each side. I smiled at her naiveté.

"No, you have to hold this so that when I get up to the top, the ladder doesn't wobble and cause me to fall." I came down and asked her to stand in front of the ladder. "Now you curl your toes at the bottom." I showed her how.

"These are my new shoes!"

"Which do you want?" I asked and laughed. "Do you want scratched shoes or a father with a broken leg?"

She wanted to run in and change shoes first, but the guests would arrive soon. Impatiently, I said, "No. Right now I don't care about your shoes. Just hold the ladder."

She held the ladder just as I had shown her. When I reached the top, however, the old bulb broke as I was unscrewing it, and the metal section stayed in the outlet. I had to climb down the ladder, hurry inside the house, turn off the breaker, and grab pliers to unscrew the metal residue.

When I went back up, Rachel faithfully held the ladder. (She didn't scuff her shoes.) As I came down, I realized the importance of what she had done. To my daughter, holding the ladder had seemed like such a meaningless chore. To me, it was a safety issue. I would not have been able to change that light if she or someone had not held my ladder.

> **The higher we need to go, the more important ladder holders become.**

As I put away my equipment, I thought, that's the way it works in the church and in the business world. The higher we need to go, the more important ladder holders become. It was one of those great moments of insight for me. I've always valued people, but in that instant, I realized the absolute necessity of seeking, recruiting, and training individuals to hold ladders or do any other leadership function. Ladder holders may feel that their contributions don't carry much weight, as my daughter did, but make no mistake—behind every high climber is a faithful ladder holder.

Since that day in Queens, the message of holding ladders has become increasingly significant to me. As I travel around the country, I sometimes ask, "Who is holding your ladder?" I'm convinced that all successful painters who can reach the highest heights of the building do so because of those below who steady them while they work and fulfill their vision.

Those who insist on doing everything themselves can still paint—but not very high, not very effectively, not very safely, and not very sensibly.

2
WHAT KIND OF PERSON IS HOLDING YOUR LADDER?

"I'm a nobody."

"I don't make any difference. No one even misses me when I'm absent."

"I just answer the telephone in our office and do a little word processing. Anybody can do what I do." "I'm not a preacher or a singer, so I'm just a lesser light in our church."

Those are the typical responses I've heard from the support people, though they are just as important in their supporting roles as the stars of the show.

I want to be clear about identifying ladder holders:
- » They are the foundation of any organization.
- » They are the ones who allow leaders to reach their highest potential.
- » They have the ladder held so securely that the leaders don't have to fret or constantly worry if they'll fall.

In the previous chapter, I asked, "Who is holding your ladder?" Now I ask, "What kind of person is holding your ladder?" Let's look more closely at those we accept, enlist, recruit, or hire to hold our ladders.

The most obvious point is we can't just throw anybody into the job. To give an idea of the importance of this role, I'll use myself as an example.

I weigh about 155 pounds and am 5 feet 8 inches, so I'm not a heavy person. Let's say you decide to climb a ladder that reaches twenty feet. I might be able to hold your ladder if the ground is totally level. What happens when you decide to ascend a forty-foot ladder? You don't want just anybody down at the bottom.

> Ladder holders are the foundation of any organization. They are the ones who allow leaders to reach their highest potential.

At conferences, I often illustrate this. I look for one of the largest men in the audience and then ask him to come up to the platform and stand next to me. I make certain he towers over me by at least six inches and weighs fifty or more pounds more than I do.

As the man stands next to me, the differences between us are too obvious to comment on. "If you were climbing a forty-foot ladder, whom would you choose to hold that ladder?" I ask the audience. Obviously, they always choose the other man.

"Look at me! I'm a great ladder holder," I say. "You don't know this, but I have a PhD in ladder holding. I love holding ladders. There's nothing I feel better about than doing just that. It gives me such deep joy and inner satisfaction. Besides that, I have learned beautiful techniques. Why, I can hold any ladder with two fingers and use only one foot. When I hold a ladder, I am so graceful that it looks as if I'm posing for a sculptor. Besides, I've held many ladders in my life. I have also held ladders in Kenya, India, and Australia, so I'm an international ladder holder. All right, a few ladders did shake a little, but so far no one has fallen—I mean, not yet."

I point to the man next to me. "You don't know anything about him, and you haven't questioned him about his experience. Yet just looking at us, you'd rather have him hold your ladder when you have to climb forty feet high. Why would you choose this less experienced person over me?"

"He's taller."

"He's stronger."

"He's bigger than you."

"We want someone strong enough to hold the ladder so we can feel safe," someone usually yells out.

I don't blame the audience. If I had a choice, I'd want someone heavier and stronger than I am at the bottom of my ladder.

The principle works in any form of leadership. Leaders call for the bigger man because their lives are on the line. The higher the climb, the stronger the person they want at the bottom. That just makes common sense.

I also discovered that the audience didn't care about my education, and they didn't want to know that I could pose gracefully while I did my job. They wanted physical strength—assurance they would be safe when they reached thirty, forty, fifty, and even sixty feet. The higher you climb, the more deliberate you must be in choosing your ladder holders. We need to pick the right people to do the job we want *done.*

NEGATIVE QUALITIES

We don't always want to pick the person who is largest. It depends on the task. Strength is important, but often we have other qualities we need. One way to see this is to focus on the qualities we don't want.

Here are the kinds of people we don't want holding our ladders.

1) We don't want those who need constant reminding.
When I know I'm going to have to make a fifty-foot climb, what kind of person do I choose? As we think about the tasks in our church or business that need to be completed, whom will we ask?

It's stressful and frustrating if we have to say to someone on Sunday morning, "Don't forget. You promised to help me Tuesday night." What a chore it is if we have to call that same person two hours before the scheduled time and say, "I just wanted to remind you that we start at 7:30 tonight."

We have many people like that in our businesses and churches. For instance, I'll tell you about a man I'll call Hector. He had the nicest smile of anyone I had ever seen. "Would you come over Friday night and help?" I once asked. He agreed and promised that he wanted to do anything he could to help me.

It didn't take me long to realize that Hector *would* do anything—that is if I reminded him enough times. This is a slight exaggeration, but it seemed that by Tuesday, I'd have to call and remind him what I wanted him to do. On Wednesday, I'd have to tell him what time I wanted him at the church. Thursday, I'd have to call again just to make sure he hadn't forgotten and planned to do something else.

> **I want to make sure that my ladder holder understands what I'm trying to accomplish.**

This doesn't apply only to Hector—the church and the marketplace are filled with people like him. As long as I make all the arrangements and explain what I need in simple detail, they'll do what I want. Some of them will come on the right day, but I can also expect them to arrive at least fifteen minutes late.

Others want to help, but I find myself having to explain every step of the process to get the job done. It's the same job I explained three weeks earlier and will need to clarify again in another three weeks.

What do we say about people like Hector?

"By the time I get through telling him, I might as well do it myself," is the common reaction.

Sometimes we're so tired of those who need constant reminding that we try to mount the steps by ourselves without any support. That's a mistake. We have focused so much on the less skilled ladder holders that we forget there are other, dependable individuals we can call on.

2) We don't want those who behave casually.

Here's a question every business and church leader should ask: "Are the people I hire or recruit intentional about their work?" If Elmer holds my ladder, will he curl all his toes and hold the ladder with both hands? Or will he have one hand draped casually across one of the rungs and a cup of Starbucks coffee in the other? Will he sip his coffee and carry on a conversation with someone across the street while I'm up there painting? I hope not. If Elmer is going to hold my ladder, I want his total attention. Distraction can mean the difference between reaching the top and crashing to the ground—headfirst and fast.

I want to make sure that my ladder holder understands what I'm trying to accomplish. Think of the various volunteer jobs in the church, such as an usher. Some years ago, I finished a conference in Albuquerque, New Mexico, on Saturday night and had planned to take the overnight flight back to Atlanta. Because of bad weather in the east, the flight was canceled, and I could not get out until midday Sunday. I picked a church to attend that morning near the hotel and went inside.

Two ushers stood in the doorway chatting about a gospel concert one of them had attended. They both held bulletins in their hands. I paused, stared at them, but they were too involved to notice me. I waited a few seconds and asked, "May I have a bulletin?" "Oh, sure," said one of them as he handed one to me and then took a step backward so that I could get through. As soon as I passed, the two men picked up their conversation. I wouldn't want either of them to hold my ladder!

What about the people in the parking lot who direct traffic? As the lot gets full, are they alert enough to help people find a space for their cars? What about the friendliness of our nursery workers? What about the minister of music or choir director? Do they care about serving or only performing?

How about the church office? Is the receptionist answering phones intentionally or casually? That is, does the receptionist make each caller feel special or act as if it's a minor intrusion on her time? Are they promptly returning voicemail messages?

Haven't most of us walked into an office and waited for several minutes while the receptionist finished a personal call? I've even had receptionists ignore me when I say, "Excuse me." Sometimes without ever looking up at me, the person behind the desk says sharply, "Just a minute." On one occasion, a woman was filing her nails and barked at me, "Can't you see I'm busy?"

When I've spoken about such situations at conferences, one or two businesspeople have approached me later and shared their own experiences with these negative qualities. They say something like, "That makes more sense for me than anything else." They realize the importance of the intentional focus of everyone in their organization. The moral of the story is: keep your eyes wide open and your ears to the ground because how we do one thing is how we do everything. The small things—every conversation, every comment, every missed deadline—matter. You should always leave room for grace, but these scenarios are valuable indicators of whether you're looking at a trustworthy ladder holder or a reckless one.

3) We don't want resumé builders.
Who are the resumé builders? They're the kinds who, while they're holding my ladder, aren't giving me their total attention. They're looking around at other things they'll do after they've finished with me. I'm only their temporary assignment until the real job comes along. They do the work—barely—but that's not their real area of interest. They're looking around for the brighter light, the shinier ladder, or the taller building. They're not committed to what they're doing now; they're thinking of what they want to do in their next position.

> As leaders, we need to choose those who are committed to us.

I want people to have their eyes on me while they hold my ladder. Too often, especially in the marketplace, those who are supposed to hold ladders are only holding on enough to appear busy. They're working, but not on the ladder. They're positioning themselves for the next job.

This means that when we select ladder holders, as leaders, we need to choose those who are committed to us. If we're going to be forty feet in the air, we don't want someone who may wave as she leaves us and moves on to hold a larger ladder down the street while we're still up in the air. Reliable ladder holders see ladder holding as their only job—the most important one—regardless of their knowledge that others are waiting for them.

4) We don't want unhappy people.
I've never understood why somebody would keep going to the same church for thirty-eight years and leave mad every Sunday. Most of us know individuals like that in our church and the marketplace. They're unhappy when they come, and they're angry when they leave. The music will be too loud one week and not lively enough the next. The pastor prayed too long or didn't preach enough gospel.

Think of a situation like this. Suppose Amos goes to the ABC Barbeque on Friday night. He tells Pastor Green they have lousy food, slow service, and high prices.

"That's terrible," Pastor Green says.

The following week, Amos says, "I ate at the ABC Barbeque again Friday night. They still have lousy food, slow service, and high prices."

Every week Amos complains about the restaurant, but he won't stop going there. Doesn't someone need to say to him, "Go somewhere else to eat?" I've often said to pastors, "Some of your members could get their healing if they just parked their car at somebody else's church."

We don't apply the same common sense to the perpetual grumblers in our congregations. They've been unhappy for forty-three years. The chances aren't very good that they'll change.

5) We don't want people to just agree.
When I was a pastor, I became aware of people who would agree with all my plans and ideas. "Oh, yes, yes, pastor," she might say. "I'll help you with the building plan. I'm here to help you with a new and more focused ministry for women, and I'll support you as you push that men's ministry." She also wants to help me with the youth choir.

Then, as the visionary leader, I started those projects. I started climbing the ladder, calmly and anxiety-free. After all, she said she'd be there to support me. I'd get up fifteen feet and look down. She wasn't there! I'd start to move upward, trying to hold things steady, and realize that the higher I climbed, the more help I needed at the bottom. I didn't know where she was, but if I could find her, I'm sure the conversation would start like this:

"You promised to hold my ladder."

"Yes, yes, of course, I'll help you. I know you're doing the right thing." Her words are empty. They make big promises but return nothing. Not only are her actions inconsistent with her words, but they indicate that she doesn't really believe what she says. As long as she says what she thinks you want to hear, she'll remain in good standing with you. In her mind, disagreement equates to being a bad employee; in reality, the opposite could be true—disagreeing and offering unique insights might actually position her as a thinker, one who is engaged in and committed to your mission.

3

FIVE CORE QUALITIES OF LADDER HOLDERS

If I'm climbing, I want to be sure that my supporters know what I'm trying to do when I'm alone at the top with my paint buckets, brushes, and scrapers. Do those on the ground understand what I'm trying to accomplish? Do they realize that I can't paint over cracked paint because I must first chip away the old? Or do they get impatient and yell, "Just put a fresh coat over the old stuff!"

I also want to make this clear: Those who are gripping the ladder don't have to agree with my tactics or methods. They do, however, need to understand where I want to go even if they would have taken a different route. They do have to believe in my vision and agree with where I'm going.

But what if they don't have the vision? What if they don't have any idea where I'm going? How much could I depend on them and their commitment to my vision?

For example, let's say I visit Joyful Tidings Church next Sunday morning and they have one hundred people in the worship service. I wait outside until the church service is over. I hold a tape recorder in my hand. As each person steps forward, I ask, "What's the vision of this church?"

> Those who are gripping the ladder don't have to agree with my tactics or methods. They do have to believe in my vision and agree with where I'm going.

How many answers will I get? Could I count on twenty people out of the one hundred to give me the same answer? I don't mean a memorized statement or something simplistic such as, "Our vision is to save souls." The church may not have an evangelistic program. Even if they did, if no one has joined the church in two years, would that still be the vision? Not likely.

If they don't know the vision, how can they be in tune with the pastor? They may love the pastor and nod appreciatively at the sermons every week. They may enjoy the music program and feel inspired by the worship. But that's still moving in the realm of projects. The sermon is a project; the music is a project. *What is the vision?*

Because I knew my vision could not be accomplished without strong ladder holders, I asked myself many times: *If I had to find a ladder holder, what core qualities would I seek?* What would they have to have for me to consider them as class A, number one, top-notch, eagle, ladder holders?

I came up with five qualities I'd insist on. There are others I'd like to see and would hope for, but these are the essentials characteristics I believe every ladder holder should possess.

The first quality is *strength*. They have to be strong. By that, I mean they must be able to handle instruction and criticism. I must be able to use plain language and not walk on eggshells and fix things for them. That means that if they need correction or re-direction in certain areas, they will implement it without my having to worry about hurting their feelings.

I'm not referring to being crass, rude, arrogant, or obnoxious. For example, let's focus on the person running the sound system. Last Sunday morning, the sound system reverberated at times and caused me to shudder. At other times, the amplification was so low that people strained to hear what I said.

I don't want excuses or lengthy explanations, and this is more important than whether the sound engineer slept well the night before. This is ministry—service to the body of Jesus Christ.

"The sound wasn't right," I need to be able to say and then add, "Do whatever you have to do to make it happen. People can't worship when they have to cover their ears with their hands."

I expect the sound engineer to know how to solve those problems. When I speak that way, I'm not trying to hurt feelings; I'm just conducting business. In the church, however, we know that some members are so fragile we can hardly correct them without upsetting them. "I'm doing my best, you know," they may say. "Why are you always picking on me? Why don't you like me? Why do you find fault in everything I do?"

We need strong ladder holders—those strong enough to take criticism and who want to do better.

To use the ladder image again, I can't be sixty feet in the air and yell down at my ladder holders to remedy the mistakes they make. I need someone strong enough to do the task right because they are attentive and secure enough to listen to me when I yell my instructions.

> **We need strong ladder holders; those strong enough to take criticism and who want to do better.**

Another way I explain this is to say, "The greater the need, the shorter the prayer." If I were drowning, I wouldn't say, "Oh God, the Everlasting Father of Abraham, Isaac, and Jacob, the Almighty One who was, is, and ever shall be, hallowed be thy name, seeth thou that I drownest? Throwest me a rope that I may cling to safely even as I am always safe in the old rugged cross."

No, I'm going to scream, "Help, God!" I won't worry about whether I addressed the entire Trinity or only Jesus. I won't be concerned about whether I concluded with "In Jesus's name. Amen." I'm too busy trying to stay alive!

Hence, the greater the need, the shorter the prayer. And when I'm up there on a forty-foot ladder, the need is great. It's not an option—I must have ladder holders who can handle instructions in two to three words and do them quickly.

The second quality is *attentiveness*. They need to pay attention, be alert to what I'm saying, and absorb it quickly. I don't want to give them the same lessons repeatedly.

Can't we assume that if James and Martha have been ushering for twenty-seven years, they ought to know what they're supposed to do? Those who clean the church ought to know where every wastebasket is. Those who sing in the choir ought to know the time they're supposed to be there to rehearse on Wednesday night and what time they're expected to be in their robes on Sunday morning.

We don't have to chase after attentive people repeatedly. They understand and respond the first time.

The third quality is *faithfulness*. I'm not referring to having faith in the Lord. That's assumed if they're serving in the church. I'm talking about having faith in me as their leader and being committed to me.

I learned very early in my own ministry that if they aren't faithful to me—if they aren't committed to the same vision I'm committed to—they'll abandon me. The worst thing is that they run away, not before I start or when I explain what I want. No, they nod, smile, and agree, but as soon as I'm fifteen feet away, they abandon me.

I need people who remain at the bottom of my ladder no matter how difficult things become. The faithful assure me that they're below as long as I'm up there. They don't need me to constantly yell, "You're doing a great job. You're wonderful!" They're steady, and I know I can count on them. They don't require constant reassurance because trust has been established—they already know where they stand because they are confident in their abilities.

The fourth quality is *firmness*. By that, I mean they don't allow manipulative people to exploit them. You can find manipulative types in every church and every corporation. Al Qaeda terrorists aren't new—only the name is. Terrorism in the church is nothing new, but it's usually cloaked in ecclesiastical language, hidden in the by-laws, or made to sound spiritual and appealing. The ultimate goal of church terrorists is control and destruction. That sounds harsh, I'm sure, but that's what they're after.

They may speak in pious language such as, "The Holy Spirit led me," or say, "The Lord spoke to my heart." They may be extremely self-deceived or just mean-spirited. It doesn't matter which because the end is the same. They want to destroy the present plans and operations. They do it in so many ways, but the one I notice most is what I call *seductive manipulation*. An illustration may help, but it's an embarrassing one.

The first time I became aware of seductive manipulation happened when I was a twenty-six-year-old assistant pastor of a church in Oregon. A few of the leaders began to call me aside. They flattered me and told me how much they admired my ministry and loved my commitment.

"You know, we really enjoy it when you preach. When you're in the pulpit, we get something out of the service," they would say and throw their arms around me. "We wish you could preach every Sunday and every Tuesday."

Until then I had never thought of such a thing. I had come to assist the senior pastor.

"You feed us when you preach or teach. You're anointed and you understand. The pastor just doesn't speak to us. His messages are all right, but they're just not relevant to our needs." The red flags were all over the place—not only were they puffing me up, but they were undermining the work and authority of the pastor. The gossip seduced me—I wanted them to like me.

This kind of conversation didn't happen just once but over a period of weeks. I was young, naïve, and egocentric. Very stupidly, I allowed their constant ego-stroking to manipulate me. Instead of faithfully holding the pastor's ladder, those conversations had my full attention. At first, I listened and thanked them. When I walked away, I'd feel really special and anointed.

It wasn't long before I participated in the conversations. "You're right. He just doesn't understand the needs of people today."

I still remember at a business meeting where there was a particularly important item on the agenda. Several of the elders who had been stroking my ego convinced me that the plan the pastor wanted to put into motion was unwise. He spoke and explained exactly what he wanted to see happen.

"May I say something?" I asked. When the pastor nodded, I stood up. I strongly disagreed with everything he had said. Point by point, I argued against what he wanted done. My seductive manipulators had done a good job.

I was wrong. I think I knew that thirty seconds after I began to speak. However, I didn't know how to back down and say, "I'm sorry." My words carried, and we vetoed something the pastor was committed to. I should have been his senior ladder holder, and I had not only waffled, but I had worked against him. I wasn't the firm assistant he deserved.

God has a way of evening things out. The following year when I was a pastor in Michigan, I reaped the fruit of the bad seed I had sown in Oregon. I was then the senior pastor, and the same type of seductive manipulators moved in on my territory.

Through that sad experience, I learned three important lessons:

1) If we disagree with our leader, we don't do so publicly. We need to discuss it with that person in private.
2) If we disagree, we ought to search our motives before we speak. We need to be sure that others don't set us

up. They won't speak up themselves, but they will find naïve and trusting souls to do the work for them.

3) If we disagree, we should be sure we don't do it for personal gain. I didn't get it at the time, but those manipulators had instilled a desire in me to become the senior pastor. Because of them, I coveted a position that God had not called me to.

As I've thought back to my behavior in Oregon, with much shame, I've realized—too late—that my agenda was not simply to disagree or express my viewpoint. My secret agenda was to look smarter, brighter, and better informed than the senior pastor. Those seductive manipulators used me just as Satan used Eve in the Garden of Eden. And just like Eve, I was too naïve to realize what was going on—until it was too late.

> If we disagree with our leader we don't do so publicly.
> If we disagree, we ought to search our motives before we speak.
> If we disagree, we should be sure we don't do it for personal gain.

The final quality is *loyalty*. I do not mean perpetual, unconditional agreement. Loyalty doesn't mean repeating, "Yes, yes, yes," no matter what the visionary says.

Three sentences describe the loyal person:
1) They may disagree with my head but not my heart.
2) They may disagree with how I do things but not why I do things.
3) They may disagree with my methods but not my motivations.

PASTOR OR CEO

When I first went to Beulah Heights Bible College as president in 1989, I didn't have a background in human resources. We had seven people on our staff at that time—four of them part-time and three full-time. (Fourteen years later, we had more than ninety people on staff.) Over the years, I've learned that those who fire and hire should prioritize those five essential qualities in a ladder holder: strength, attentiveness, faithfulness, firmness, and loyalty.

> Even though they are both pastor and CEO, they can't be both at the same time.

Although my experience has been largely with personnel at Beulah Heights Bible College, these principles carry through in pastoral situations as well. Almost any week in the year, I have conversations with pastors who have problems with paid staff. They have a difficult job today. On one hand, they are pastors—that means they're shepherds who care for the sheep. On the other hand, they are the Chief Executive Officers (CEOs) and the congregation holds them responsible for smoothly running the church's business.

The first thing I've learned is that even though they are both pastor and CEO, they can't be both at the same time. I try to help them understand the difference between the two and when to give priority to one and when to give it to the other.

It may help if I explain it this way. Let's say I'm the senior minister at First Spiritual Church. To every paid staff member, I am the CEO first and the pastor second. That means I must first do the business of the church with them. When I have accomplished that, I can function as their pastor. If I get the order wrong, I am in trouble, and so is the organization.

> We hire people for *what* they know; we fire them for *who* they are.

To every church member, I am the pastor first and the CEO second. I must be able to reach out to them as those who need to be nurtured, strengthened, encouraged, rebuked, and disciplined. When I've performed my pastoral duties, I can function as the CEO. If I get this wrong, then I've put projects before people. If I see the members only as the means to accomplish what I want done, then I'll manipulate, threaten, coerce, or flatter them into fulfilling my agenda.

When I function as CEO with paid employees, the first lesson I've learned is to hire people for *what* they know and fire them for *who* they are.

We may hire the musician because she can make the simplest music sound like a concerto in every piece she plays. We fire her because she has a bad attitude. We hire an office manager because he is a computer whiz and understands spreadsheets, profit and loss, government regulations, and knows all the latest software. We fire him because he can't get along with people.

What do we do when it's time to put someone on staff? I believe we need to re-think our policy on what really makes a good ladder holder. We want competent people, obviously. But when we select ladder holders, we need to spend more time studying and learning who they are rather than what they know.

> **Hire slowly and fire quickly. Don't rush hiring decisions; don't delay firing decisions.**

I can read their resumés and I can talk to people they've worked for and with. That is important. But I also know that troubles in the job usually start over personality issues and not over competency. Once hired, they will give me joy or grief. With few exceptions, the people I have fired I have terminated because of their attitudes. Rarely have I had to get rid of someone for lack of ability to do the job. Skills can be taught; character cannot.

This leads me to the second lesson I've learned:

Hire slowly and fire quickly.

It's better to have a vacancy than to have bad help. Suppose the doctor diagnoses you with cancer, says surgery is the only option, and asks, "When would you want it scheduled?"

I'm guessing you'd say, "As soon as possible."

As a leader, a good question to ask ourselves is: Why do I tolerate incompetent staff? Why do I allow them to infect the rest of the staff with their bad attitude? I like to say it this way: Don't rush hiring decisions; don't delay firing decisions.

The third lesson I've learned is this: *The best time to fire somebody is the first time it goes through your head.* We tend to get our roles confused again here. Instead of thinking as a CEO for the good of the organization, we tend to switch to our pastoral role and excuse or overlook problems serious enough that we'd consider terminating them if we were only honest with ourselves.

I've also learned that if the situation is serious enough to fire people and we don't, we begin to search for reasons to keep them.

About the time I figured out this third lesson, I spotted an advertisement in USA Today by Randall Murphy, the founder and president of the Acclivus Corporation. I don't know much about Acclivus except that their clients include major organizations such as Dunn and Bradstreet, Exxon, Mobile, Dell, FedEx, Dr. Pepper/Seven-Up and Roadway Express. The ad read: "When you are assigned the task of taking the hill-or the market-you are less concerned about who is *for* you and more concerned about who is *with* you."[1]

Those words impacted me, and I read the sentence several times. I've translated Murphy's statement into the business of the church, such as when a congregation starts a new building program.

Those who make pledges are *for* us; those who pay their pledges are *with* us. We don't have to be involved with churches very long before we recognize that there is a large gap between those two groups.

Just because people say, "I'm for you," isn't the real issue. The real issue is the evidence of their pledge. Do they do what they promise? Do they faithfully follow their words by their actions?

> The best time to fire somebody is the first time it goes through your head. ... If the situation is serious enough to fire people and we don't, we begin to search for reasons to keep them.

THREE LEVELS OF LADDER HOLDERS

I've already mentioned the five things we have to look for to identify our ladder holders. From there, I started thinking about what happens with ladder holders in a church and discovered that not all ladder holders are created equal because not all have the same strengths. The implications are far-reaching—you can be great at what you do and still be an ineffective ladder holder, depending on what kind of ladder holder you are. Even worse, you can sacrifice what you love and excel at on the altar of holding a ladder you were never meant to hold.

I have concluded that there are three levels of ladder holders.

First, there are the *followers*. This word can refer to everybody in the congregation.

Second are the *ministers*. They feel God has called them, empowered them, and gifted them to serve in the church. When I use the word minister, I don't mean ordained ministers and pastors, although it may include them. Rather, ministers refer to all of those with a heart to serve others.

Third are *leaders*. They minister through others. They don't have only a sense of calling; they also have passion, and that passion is to see God work through others. True leaders don't try to deceive themselves into thinking they can or even want to do everything. They're willing to empower and trust others. Ministers do service primarily by themselves; leaders do service through others.

Throughout my years of serving in the church, we have ruined many good ministers by shoving them into leadership. For example, let's say that Josh has a passion for prison ministry because he is gifted in connecting with the incarcerated. They listen to him because they trust him. On his own and without anyone from the church behind him, Josh goes to the local jail every Friday and Saturday. He does this out of concern and love. He carries gospel portions with him and teaches prisoners how to read the New Testament. He sings, he preaches, and he takes time to counsel anyone who asks him to.

> Those who make pledges are **for** us; those who pay their pledges are **with** us. We don't have to be involved with churches very long before we recognize that there is a large gap between those two groups.

After two years, Josh has achieved remarkable outcomes, including leading several people to believe in Jesus Christ. Some of them have joined the church. Everyone recognizes the value of Josh's ministry.

One day the pastor says, "We need to start an official prison ministry through our church. Josh is already doing it, so let's put him in charge."

"Every time we take prayer requests," an elder says, "Josh asks us to pray for the prison ministry and the prisoners."

"He regularly sends e-mails about the people who got saved," says a deacon.

"He's passionate about it," says one. The board agrees unanimously.

That decision may sound like a good idea, but in the ten minutes they took to make that official verdict, they ruined Josh and his ministry.

Remember the three ladder holders:
1) *Followers*. This word can refer to everybody in the congregation.
2) *Ministers*. They feel God has called them, empowered them, and gifted them to serve.
3) *Leaders*. They minister through others.

Until then, Josh had been an excellent minister for God. He did an outstanding job as long as he was the only one who did the work. He has a tender heart, and people instinctively trust him.

But now, his ministry has been ruined because Josh has moved from ministry to leadership. He's no longer person-centered. He's overwhelmed with recruiting musicians and evangelists. He's constantly scheduling who will go to which jail and at what time. He must spend an immense amount of time teaching those who have volunteered for ministry and need to understand appropriate behavior and what they can and can't do for the prisoners. He has to explain, for instance, that they can't carry mail in or out for those incarcerated. They can't give advice, especially not legal advice. Several times, he has had to go to the sheriff and apologize for mistakes his people have made.

After four months, Josh realizes that is no longer a minister, but a manager and leader. His passion starts to dry up. The well-meaning church board has ruined him.

He's pouring his efforts into holding the ladder for others, but he needs to be climbing his own ladder.

Even though people like Josh excel in ministry doesn't mean they can function well as good ladder holders.

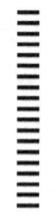 Ministers do service primarily by themselves; leaders do service through others.

TRAINING LADDER HOLDERS

This leads me to emphasize that ladder holders need to be *trained*. Very few ministers have qualified and trained ladder holders. I've held conversations with pastors of large churches all over this country. I point out the qualities I've already mentioned. They need people who are strong, attentive, faithful, firm, and loyal.

Then I say, "Name your ladder holders. I'm not asking for positions and titles such as deacons or trustees. Think about those five qualities I gave you." I pause and then say, "Tell me the names of your ladder holders."

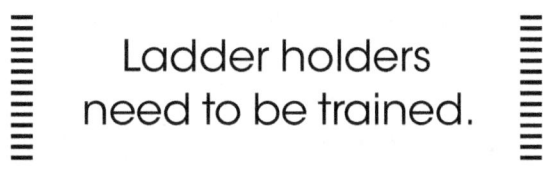

Ladder holders need to be trained.

No matter how many times I've done this, five is the most anyone has been able to name. The size of the congregation doesn't seem to matter, whether it's a church of one hundred members or more than 10,000.

When the pastors can't get beyond a few names, it tells me that the church has done an excellent job of raising followers but an abysmal job with leadership development.

At the beginning of this book, I mentioned that developing people takes time, and time is one thing we don't have in our busy lives. Time scarcity is the low-hanging fruit of excuses for procrastinating or failing to develop people altogether. Time is our most precious commodity, and we simply can't afford to lose it. Unfortunately, this mindset is a trap. The truth is, you may not *like* to lose time you could have spent doing other things that seem more urgent, but you can't afford *not* to treat developing your people as the most urgent.

I also remind pastors that their armor bearers or assistants may not necessarily be ladder holders. Just because somebody is an assistant pastor, assistant choir director, vice president of the corporation, or has an impressive title doesn't make him or her a trusted ladder holder.

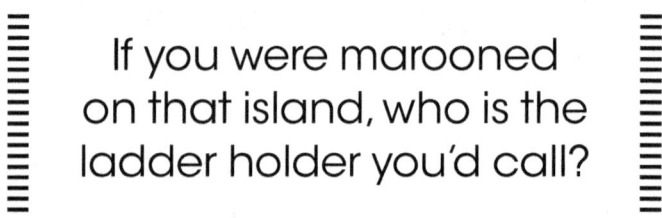

If you were marooned on that island, who is the ladder holder you'd call?

To make this clear, I try to get pastors to think of situations when the church is filled with problems and ask, "To whom would you turn for help?"

They still stare at me in confusion, so here's an illustration that seems to clarify what I mean.

"Let's say you are marooned on an island. The battery on your cell phone is running low. You decide you have just enough juice to make one call. Let's also say that you know that no member of your family is available." Then I pause and ask, "Whom will you call?"

Without fail they can easily eliminate the ones they *wouldn't* call—and some of them are prominent in the church—but they can't name someone they *would* call. This exercise has brought many to realize that they need a true ladder holder—a person who is faithful and committed to them personally. Those are the individuals who will do whatever is necessary to get them off the island.

4
HOW DO WE RECRUIT VOLUNTEERS?

"Who will hold my ladder?" That's a common way for us to get help. We look around, cry out to whoever will come to our aid, and welcome them, regardless of their abilities. We may not put it that way. Instead, we announce, "We need two new Sunday school teachers. Who will serve for one year?" Or we plead for men to join the choir. That method works! People volunteer and we get results. There's just one serious problem—it's the wrong approach.

My advice is simple. *Stop asking for volunteers.*

When I was a pastor and asked for volunteers, the people who couldn't do the job always raised their hands. I appreciated their zeal, but they simply couldn't do what I needed to be done.

How do we un-volunteer a volunteer?

People who couldn't sing rushed to join the choir. People who had forgotten how to smile volunteered to usher. People who disliked children raised their hands to keep the nursery. People who couldn't teach committed themselves to take a Sunday school class. I also realized another problem. Within a short time, those who volunteer so readily are just as ready to un-volunteer. They seem to hear the Holy Spirit whisper "I send you" every time the pastor calls for help. After a few weeks, they also seem to hear the same Holy Spirit whisper, "Your work here is finished." Not that they accomplished anything productive, but at least they left. In reality, they shouldn't have volunteered in the first place.

The bigger problem occurs when those inept but well-meaning helpers get into their position, and then we have to ask, "How do you get rid of them?"

That is the question; that is also the problem. How do we un-volunteer a volunteer? There isn't much chance that the bass in the choir who can't hit a C below middle C will ever learn. The grumbling nursery staff person won't suddenly love to change diapers.

Suppose we read the headline in tomorrow's newspaper that says the local public schools seek volunteers to teach English, science, and math. Would I want my children to attend a school where all instructors are volunteers?

The public wouldn't stand for it. "We want professionals teaching our children," they would insist.

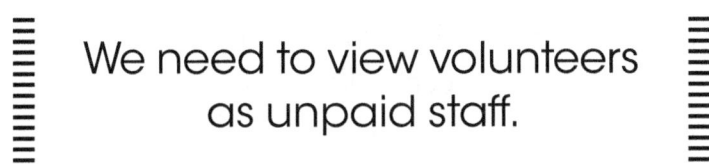

Why do we staff our Christian Education departments, our ushering committees, and our nurseries with volunteers? Could it be that reading, writing, and arithmetic are a lot more important than real life issues, such as preparing for heaven or personal integrity? We keep doing what the church has been doing for the past hundred years: we print notices in the bulletin, the newsletter, and on the church's website: "we need four teachers for the children's department."

Surely there must be a better way. And there is!

We need to view volunteers as unpaid staff.

I've come to the conclusion that the most qualified people are waiting to be recruited. They don't rush to sign up on the legal pad hanging on a bulletin board. They don't call the worship leader's cell phone. They're there, available, and they're willing to serve *if they're asked*. We need to learn how to recruit volunteers.

THE BIBLE AND VOLUNTEERS

Have you ever wondered what the Bible says about volunteerism?

From the time of the Old Testament all the way up to John the Baptist, followers generally chose their leader. People would hear a great prophet, listen to him, do whatever he told them, and become his disciple.

Something changed, however, after John the Baptist. The next leader on the world scene was Jesus. Followers didn't choose Jesus; Jesus chose followers. I wonder how many people think about that. Each gospel account tells us how Jesus went about his ministry. One of His first acts was to choose those He wanted to follow Him, and they were the ones He trained. (See Mark 1:16-20 and Luke 5:1-11.)

> Followers didn't choose Jesus; Jesus chose followers.

Sometimes people offered to follow Jesus and He turned them down. Here are two examples:

A certain man said unto him, Lord, I will follow thee whithersoever thou goest. And Jesus said unto him, Foxes have holes and birds of the air have nests, but the Son of Man hath not where to lay his head.—Luke 9:57-58

Jesus said no.

Another time, Jesus set a man free from demons, and afterward, the healed man wanted to go with the Lord. Jesus said no. (See Mark 5:18-19.)

Jesus held a powerful vision of his ladder that stretched from earth to heaven. He didn't want just anyone supporting him. In fact, just before his betrayal, Jesus said to his disciples: "Ye have not chosen me, but I have chosen you, and ordained you, that ye should go and bring forth fruit, and *that* your fruit should remain" (John 15:16a).

At no place in Jesus's ministry do we read that he stood up and said, "I need helpers to do the work. I want fifty people to follow me." Instead, Jesus recruited volunteers who would hold that ladder firm no matter how hard the forces of evil struck.

Instead of seeking people to volunteer, wise leaders follow the Lord's example and seek out the gifted. As a pastor and president of a growing Bible college, I know that I must find people gifted in all the key positions if we're going to be successful. Yes, I've made mistakes, but I've made many good decisions, too. I watch for those who show that "extra something"—call it a gift or a unique quality—but there are individuals who have that special spark that sets them apart. Those are the ones I want to develop. Every church and every organization has them. If you don't know who they are, you're missing something.

In the New Testament, Paul writes about spiritual gifts several times. Although he lists nine of them in 1 Corinthians 12, he doesn't give the entire catalog of abilities. Obviously, there are gifts he didn't mention, but the point is the same. If we want something to happen, we rely on those who are talented, gifted, and can make it happen. We don't sit around and hope they'll knock on our doors. Like Jesus did, we go after them and say, "We want you. We have a place for you."

It's also interesting that those Jesus recruited had to decide if they wanted to follow him, even after they were asked. In Luke 9:59-62, Jesus asked a man to follow Him. The man protested that he had to go home and bury his father. Jesus said, "Let the dead bury their dead: but go thou and preach the kingdom of God" (v.60).

> And another also said, "Lord, I will follow thee; but let me first go bid them farewell, which are at home at my house." And Jesus said unto him, No man, having put his hand to the plough, and looking back, is fit for the kingdom of God—vv. 61-62.

It's also interesting that Paul exhorts the Thessalonians, "And we beseech you, brethren, to know them which labour among you, and are over you in the Lord, and admonish you" (1 Thessalonians 5:12). The only time I hear anyone quote that verse is during ordination services. That fits, of course, but it has a much wider application.

In the first chapter of this book, I pointed out three ways to do the work of the church and the third is to develop others—to teach them to do what they can do. I also pointed out that it takes time for that to happen. It means working with those ladder holders and instructing them on how to do an excellent job. Some may be best at holding short ladders and others taller ones. Some may work best alone and others in groups. The principle still remains the same: leaders need to develop others, and doing so requires an ongoing process of mutual labor and relationship building. A second principle is equally important—while we don't want the wrong people holding our ladders, we should be careful not to disqualify those who are simply inexperienced. As leaders, it is our responsibility to engage our team, even those who may not appear to be cut out for the job. Ability and talent are important, but not at the expense of neglecting the heart and eagerness to serve. You may find that with a little training and investment, they may be the best ladder holders you'll ever have as their latent gifts begin to surface. This guideline becomes especially important as your team expands.

I know that in larger congregations, it becomes difficult for the pastors to know everyone. By the time a church has

10,000 members, the senior pastor probably doesn't know more than 10 percent of them. It simply means they have many ladders and many painters, and they need an even larger support force behind those painters.

> **Wise leaders assimilate people by recognizing their gifts and placing them in the right role.**

True leaders develop their own followers—I'll say more about that in the next chapter. Wise leaders assimilate people by recognizing their gifts and work ethic and placing them in the right role. They have files on who can do what function. When we need chaperones to go with our youth group on a field trip, if we're smart, we don't send out a call and ask, "Who's going to help?" Just because they are parents doesn't mean they would make appropriate chaperones.

There may be those who don't have the time or inclination to work with the youth department every week. But if we know their capabilities and call on them two or three times a year when we have special events going on, they're likely to say, "Yes, I can help."

It's not a hopeless task to find out who is talented. With great computer programs available, when we do intake we can do a gifts inventory, we can do the passion inventory, or a calling inventory.

When a new member says, "I love organizing short-term projects," that's important for us to put on file. When we get ready to put out a new church directory, for example, that's a short-term project.

That person can organize and make the operation run smoothly. That is the same person who won't be available for tasks that go on every week throughout the year. The first step to identifying your ladder holders is to pay attention and listen.

Here's an example. I spoke at a leadership conference in Boston at the New Covenant Christian Church where Bishop Gilbert Thompson, a visionary, is the senior pastor. Bishop Thompson sat in the front row with an open laptop, typing notes as fast as he could. He didn't want to miss any significant information. I remember seeing the smile on his face when I talked about not asking for volunteers.

> We need different ladder holders for different levels of ministry.

Months later Bishop Thompson's assistant said that one significant factor "has revolutionized our ministry. We don't ask for volunteers anymore-—we recruit them."

Is it any wonder that New Covenant Christian Church has dozens of high-level ladders up?

IMPORTANT ISSUES, IMPORTANT RECRUITING

Think about volunteers this way. You are a leader. You're only four feet off the ground, but you're climbing the rungs. As you gaze upward, you know you're capable of reaching a height of at least sixty feet.

As you start to ascend, are you going to cry out, "People of God, someone—anyone—come and hold this ladder?" Not likely. If you're a wise leader, you will already have chosen (or recruited) someone you trust. You want to reach as high as your ladder will go and not worry whether the person at the bottom is going to lose interest or walk away.

When we're training ladder holders, those learners need clear instruction. Church folk don't take hints, and the best way to understand this is to think about church announcements—while they are important, they truth is that at the end of the day, they remain insufficient.

As leaders, we can put all the information in the bulletin and the newsletter. We can tell them individually in person, make phone calls, send out e-mails, proclaim it from the pulpit, and write an announcement for the overhead or PowerPoint. It doesn't matter what we do or how often we send out the information, people will still phone the church office. "What time was that meeting? Was it nine or nine-thirty? Was it Monday or Tuesday?"

When we're developing ladder holders, however, we train them the right way. A good way to look at this is from the book of Proverbs. Although much of the instruction reads as if it's a father advising a son, scholars have seen this differently. The advice and instruction are intended for scholars in training. The instructors looked upon them as students or sons. These are instructions for personal growth and leadership.

The oft-quoted Proverbs 22:6 (NKJV) reads: "Train up a child in the way he should go, And when he is old he will not depart from it." If we apply this (and I think this is the right way) to students or scholars receiving instructions, it means that if we who are leaders train new people properly—that is, when we do it right and do it in the beginning—we'll produce the right kind of results. It also means we won't have to take a lot of correctional action later. If a tree starts growing right the first time, we don't have to spend all kinds of time trying to nourish and grow it. Ladder holders must be properly trained and developed promptly. The effort you invest now will pay off in the future.

BEFORE CLIMBING LADDERS

Joseph Campbell once said that one of the great tragedies in life is to climb to the top of the ladder only to find that our ladder is leaning against the wrong wall. He meant that too many people take what he called the prudent path in life and yet they miss the joy. He said they never discover their bliss.

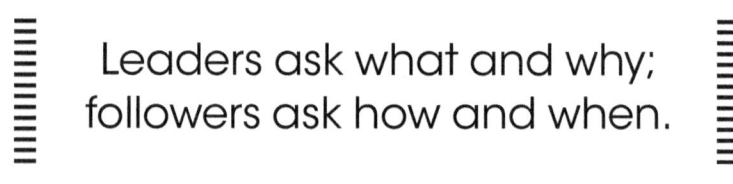
Leaders ask what and why; followers ask how and when.

How do we avoid that problem? How do we help ourselves and others discover our bliss?

Before we start climbing, we have to do three things:

1) *We need to decide where we want to go.*
We need to be sure of our reason for being on the ladder in the first place. What tools do we need to do the job for which we're climbing the ladder? What tools will we need when we get up there? One thing I learned during my student days when I painted was that it was just too tiring and time-consuming to go up and down that ladder. I had to make sure I had everything ready before I started up.

2) *We need to be clear about our vision.*
We need to be able to tell our ladder holders why we're up there and why they're working hard. If we get really high and the ladder sways, we had better be sure we know why we're there. When we go through those turbulent times—and we all do—we'd better be clear about our reason for being so high off the ground. We also need to make it clear to those who support us so that they'll know why they're doing their jobs. We have to know that the pay-off is worth the treachery and risk often involved in climbing high.

Leaders ask two questions. I mentioned this in my book *Futuring*[2], but I think it's important to say it again here.

Leaders ask *what* and *why*; followers ask *how* and *when*. Every effective leader needs to understand this.

Leaders must first define the what—that which they want done. Once they know that answer they need to be clear on why: Why are we doing this?

I gave this illustration in *Futuring*.[3] At Beulah Heights Bible College, we wanted to reach out and start a curriculum for students for whom English was not their first language. The curriculum was the *what*.

Why did we want to do that? Because the mission of the institution, even in its earliest days, was to reach unreached groups. *Why?* There are increasingly large numbers of people for whom English is a second language and we need to reach them. *Why?* Because they represent another market. *Why?* Because the place of missions has changed. There are more other-country-born missionaries in America today than there are missionaries from America in other countries. *Why?* Because they don't have to get visas and they have naturally built bridges, their credibility is in place, and their language is in place.

> 3) *We need to ask ourselves: what are we doing to prepare ourselves as better communicators?*

During the summer breaks when I was a student at Beulah Heights Bible College, I earned my living as a painter. I've always said that I did it to pay my bills and not because it was my idea of a higher calling.

Before we start climbing, we have to do three things:
1) We need to decide where we want to go.
2) We need to be clear about our vision.
3) We need to ask ourselves: What are we doing to prepare ourselves as better communicators?

I remember many times I'd get tired of moving up and down. The first few days I'd forgotten a tool or realized I needed something else and would have to go back down to get it. That was both tiring and inefficient.

Because I learned that lesson quite well, I teach it this way at conferences. I'll often ask the audience if any have done professional painting. Two or three people usually raise their hands, so I ask them to join me.

"Pretend I'm going to paint the second story of a house," I say to them. "It's way up there, the paint is peeling, and it's in pretty bad shape. I'm getting ready to go up on a forty-foot ladder. I don't want to go up and down repeatedly, so tell me what I need in my tool belt before I go up."

"You'll need a scraper and wire brush," one will say.

"You'll need sandpaper and a hammer."

One of them will mention a nail setter because there are always nails poking out. Someone will mention a caulking gun.

"You'll need paint and a brush and at least one rag to wipe away any smears you make," one of them will say.

I smile because they have it exactly right. "Now, imagine you're climbing a forty-foot ladder as a Sunday school teacher, and you want to be excellent at it. What tools do you need in your tool belt?"

Then I ask, "Are there any Sunday school teachers here? Come on up." After they come up—and there are always a lot of them—I ask, "Are you a good Sunday school teacher?"

Besides smiles and a few giggles, they answer, "Yes."

"Can you become a better Sunday school teacher?"

The answer is always, "Yes!"

"What do you have to do to become a better Sunday school teacher?" Then I wait for them to respond.

They always start with "I need to pray more, and I need to read the Bible more."

Everyone nods and I say, "Yes, that's good, but what else do you need to do?" Before the teachers respond, people from the audience yell out, "Read more books."

I ask them to name a few books, and they do. Then they start adding things such as a concordance, a Bible dictionary, a Bible encyclopedia, and different versions of the Bible.

We could ask the same questions for any position in the church. What I want them to think about is this: What must I do if I'm going to be a better, more effective communicator?

I also remind church leaders that whenever we get up to preach, we need to remind ourselves that we have five generations facing us, so there are a few questions that leaders must ask themselves.

How effective are we at reaching them? For us to be more effective, what are we putting in our toolkits to improve our communication skills, storytelling skills, movement, hand gestures, body language, and vocabulary? What are we reading that puts us in touch with the younger generations? A deep understanding of how each generation perceives and adapts to evolving leadership patterns and trends holds the key to answering these questions.

LEADERSHIP ISSUE	SENIORS	BUILDERS	BOOMERS	BUSTERS (GEN-X)	MOSAICS (NEXTERS)
Era Born	Before 1928	1929-1945	1946-1964	1965-1983	1984-X
Life Paradigm	Manifest Destiny	Be grateful you have a job	You owe me	Relate to me	Life is a cafeteria
Attitude toward Authority	Respect	Endure	Replace	Ignore	Choose
Role of Relationships	Long-term	Significant, useful	Limited, caring	Central	Global
Value System	Traditional	Conservative	Self-based	Changing	Shop around
Role of Career	Loyal, responsible	Means for living	Central focus	Irritant	Always changing
Schedules	What's up?	Mellow	Frantic	Aimless	Volatile
Technology	What's that?	Hope to outlive it	Master it	Enjoy it	Employ it
View of the Future	Uncertain	Seek to stabilize	Create it!	Hopeless	??

It's also important to remind ourselves that not everyone is a leader. God doesn't call all of us to it. Many of us know that intellectually, yet some of us in leadership positions often try to fulfill jobs we're not suited for.

Maybe we need to become managers.

5

ARE WE MANAGING LADDERS?

Are you a leader? Or has God gifted you to be a manager? It is important to figure out which one we are and where we belong.

Leaders tend to know how high they'd like to climb, but sometimes, the destination is so high that those next to them don't always see it as clearly as they do because it's out of their line of vision.

Managers know exactly where to position the ladder for maximum benefit. They may not see that special spot that leaders do, but they can figure out how to make everything work so leaders can ascend the steps and not have to look back and worry if they have solid support.

First, I want to make it clear that leaders aren't superior, and neither are managers. One is not more important than the other; however, they are different. The grid below distinguishes between leaders and managers. We need managers just as surely as we need leaders.

LEADERS	MANAGERS
Emphasize what and why	Emphasize how and when
Work from the future back to the present	Work from the past to the present
Focus on the long-term	Focus on the short-term or immediate
Embrace a macro-perspective	Embrace a micro-perspective
Favor innovative thinking	Favor routine/safe thinking
Seek to balance idealism with realism	Emphasize pragmatism over idealism
Show revolutionary flair	Protect status quo
Clarify the vision, inspire, and motivate	Implement the vision
Excite others by change	Are threatened by change
Decide quickly	Decide slowly
Identify opportunities	Identify obstacles
Take risks	Avoid risks
Pursue resources	Actions limited to available resources
People-centered	System-centered
Idea-centered	Plan-centered
Centered on core issues	Distracted by peripheral issues
Want others' approval	Need others' approval
Do the right thing	Do things right

No matter how great and visionary leaders are, unless they have managers on their team, they won't get very far.

Second, we need to recognize which one we are, because if we're leaders in a manager's position, we become frustrated and ineffective. We'll constantly see better ways to do things or lose patience with those who methodically work out details. Just as true, if we're managers in a leader's position, we're killing our organization. We're busy seeing that things function properly, ensuring that all lights are put out at night, and making certain that we don't overpay our creditors. If that's where we are, we don't have the time, energy, or ability to dream about the future.

If we're managers, we pride ourselves on being practical.

By contrast, if we're leaders, we pride ourselves on being imaginative and visionary.

OBSERVATIONS ABOUT LEADERS AND MANAGERS

- » Leaders and managers complement each other.
- » Both need to work in the area of their strength.
- » Successful managers aren't always successful leaders.
- » Successful leaders aren't always successful managers.
- » We must evaluate the success of managers differently from the success of leaders.
- » We consider managers successful when they operate the organization efficiently as well as deliver services on time and within budget.
- » We consider leaders successful when they enable their organization to grow in its ability to serve the community by discovering new needs, expanding the resource base, and innovating approaches to service delivery, and when they energize or transform the organization.

Third, if we're supervisors in charge of people, we want to figure out the kind of ladder holders we need. Sometimes a situation calls for another leader and sometimes a manager. If we're leaders, we'll learn to recognize individual gifts. You can refer to my book, *Futuring*[4] if you would like to take a deeper dive into this topic.

Here's an interesting difference between leaders and managers. Leaders focus on the future. They know what they want to accomplish; they can see five years into the future. They work from the future back to the present to show others how to get to the fulfillment of their vision.

> Leaders know where they want to reach. Managers know exactly where to position the ladder for the maximum benefit.

Managers just don't see life that way. They conceptualize by working from the past to get to the present. They know how things used to operate. They've learned what works and what doesn't work. They've observed disaster, and they've observed success, and now their primary goal is to adjust the present based on past mistakes and capitalize on past achievements. Now, they build on the past to work efficiently in the present. They have no guidelines to take them into the future.

Let's see how this works on a practical level. Let's say we decide that we're going to have a banquet to honor our pastor's ten years of service to our congregation. If you are a gifted manager, you will ask, "How did you do this before? What did you do on his fifth anniversary as pastor?" Or the manager might go to the files and church archives to find out how the church did it for the previous pastor, who served almost thirty years. The managers will soon know exactly what time and what activities occurred. They'll know who spoke, where they held the banquet, how much they charged members, and even have a copy of the menu. Managers know the past, so they can tweak it to make it flow with the present.

> If we're managers, we pride ourselves on being practical.
>
> If we're leaders, we pride ourselves on being imaginative and visionary.

If we give the same task to a leader, that person will start at a different place. "Forget five years ago. This is now. What's the purpose of this event? What do we want to see accomplished? What is the outcome we want from this banquet?"

Leaders will also ask, "Is this the best time to do this? Who do we need to call in to help us make this happen?"

Once they've established where they want to be at the end of the banquet, they work backward.

> Leaders focus on the future. They work from the future back to the present to show others how to get to the fulfillment of their vision.
>
> Managers conceptualize by working from the past to get to the present.
>
> They build on the past to work efficiently in the present.

Here's another way of understanding leaders. They embrace a macro-perspective or the big picture;

managers embrace a micro-perspective or a snapshot. It's difficult for managers to see anything that isn't on their desk. They focus on narrow, specific tasks—that's why they're good managers.

If we switch managers into leaders' roles, everything stalls. If we try to make leaders into managers, they can't take their eyes off the skies long enough to figure out how to strengthen the ladder or position all the people they need—a task that requires future-forward thinking and strategizing.

Leaders need to understand—especially those at the CEO or senior pastor level—that one of the greatest challenges they are going to continue to face is painting the large picture.

They also know that even when others have some *traits* of a leader—namely, the tendency to look ahead—they still don't always grasp the breadth and depth of the leader's vision. They may say, "Okay, there's one house on the prairie. Yes, that's nice." But, the leader wants them to see the larger canvas that also includes mountains in the background and streams in the foreground. Leaders may want people to see the cumulous clouds that drift across the landscape, but viewers, even forward-thinking ones, may see only the glint of the sun's rays on the gently flowing stream.

Leaders understand that. In fact, with the help of managers, they form groups of stream gazers and house viewers; however, leaders continue to take in the broader picture they've painted. Leaders favor innovative thinking; they're full of new ideas. They constantly push the boundaries, eager to try new programs or envision exciting opportunities.

Managers favor routine thinking. They want to know exactly what's expected of them and they'll do it faithfully. "You want me to hold the left side of this huge ladder?" they ask. "You bet! And no one will ever grip it more firmly than I will."

> If we switch managers into leaders' roles, everything stalls. If we try to make leaders into managers, they can't take their eyes off the skies long enough to figure out how to strengthen the ladder or position all the people they need.

Managers don't have many original ideas. Leaders have a revolutionary flair and constantly turn things over, around, and upside down. Managers protect the status quo, and they hold on. Change is difficult for managers. If you have put a manager in a department where you want to bring about change and improvement, you will be disappointed because they will maintain the present system and operations—perhaps more efficiently—but they won't transform the atmosphere. Because of the opposing strengths of the leader and manager, they must commit to clear communication, alignment on vision and goals, established boundaries and roles, and developing a foundation of mutual respect. Those elements will be the difference between contentious and effective collaboration.

As I've already pointed out, for leaders, the emphasis is on *what* and *why*; for managers, the emphasis is on *how* and *when*. Someone has said it this way: Those who know how will always work for those who know why.

Leaders inspire, and they're quick to challenge and urge people to try new things. Managers control; they direct attention and activities. If we could see this as God's plan for church growth and that God needs both types, it could bring a lot of harmony into the way we put up and guard our ladders.

We need both. I often think that when we talk about leadership, we make managers come across as less significant. One of the most valuable qualities I see in managers is their proficiency in keeping the painter's feet solidly on the ladder. Some visionaries are so caught up in their vision they think they can walk on air or leap from building to building. Managers remind them of their human limitations.

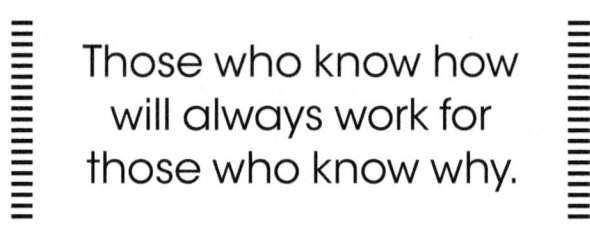

> Those who know how will always work for those who know why.

Managers also guard tradition—and all not tradition is bad. Many times, the tradition is the framework, the solid foundation that we can never abandon if we want to keep our feet on the solid rock. We have only to think of leaders who have reached magnificent heights and then fallen to the ground or hung on helplessly until someone stepped in to stabilize them, placing their feet firmly on the first rung to support their journey back up the ladder.

On a personal level, I'm one of those visionary types, but God has given me a team with some managers. They remind me I'm earthbound when I want to fly into outer space. I'm also smart enough to listen to them. At times, I've also had to push them. On several occasions, they had reservations, but they trusted me and my vision. That's how God wants it to work, isn't it?

> **Change excites leaders and it frightens managers. We need both. Healthy fear is an ally.**

Let's see how this works in the church. Let's say Dr. Holmes, the CEO and pastor, has a powerful vision to build a big building. That's inspiring, but unless he has controls in place, he'll constantly be over budget and over time. Dr. Holmes started with the sanctuary that would cost two million dollars, but his vision kept getting larger. He kept changing, seeing more efficient ways to reach larger numbers of people, to train more effectively, and to guide more troubled souls into the kingdom. His final vision is for a nine-building complex that will cost eighty million dollars. Chaos will take over unless a good manager brings in stability and control.

It's also true that change excites leaders, and it frightens managers. We need both in an enterprise like that. Healthy fear is an ally.

Whenever we talk about modifications or adjustments, here's an important fact to remember: The one who proposes those changes is not the same as the person who is listening to the plans. If we put them both on a page, we'd have a line down the middle and they would be in two different columns.

If we draw a line through the middle of the page, the left-side column would be what I call the gain column; the right-hand column is what I call the loss column. When Pastor Holmes speaks to people and tells them about the changes, he's talking about the gain column. He emphasizes the good things that will come out of his ideas and projects. He won't tell them about the possibilities of failure or create doubts in their minds.

However, suppose a single parent, Minnie Thomas, is listening. She can only think of the losses. The warmth and closeness of members will be gone. She used to be able to make appointments to talk to Bishop Holmes, but she won't be able to do that anymore. He says they'll have a full-time counselor, but Minnie Thomas wants the bishop.

> Leaders identify opportunities; managers identify obstacles.

Behind her sits Elder Kenny Sams. He's been a member of that church for fifty-one years. He was baptized there at age sixteen. Tears fill his eyes when he realizes that the old baptismal tank will be gone. He and his wife were married there, and his wife's funeral was held in that building. Now all of that will be gone.

Dr. Holmes's business manager, Ezra Bird, currently has a corner office, but he knows from the new building plans that he'll now be stuck in an office with two windows that face another building. He also knows that his new office will measure six square feet less than his previous one. He's not excited about the change. He can see only loss.

When we talk about church growth we're talking about gain, but as the church grows, those who are actively involved may easily view that as a loss. Their influence, power, and control are eroded. Individuals with greater talents, stronger motivation, and more expertise will come in. Leaders need to understand that and pre-emptively address those concerns when they want to make things different. They themselves are excited about change, but managers are threatened. Leaders move quickly; managers move slowly. It is vital that leaders do more than just communicate upcoming changes—they must level with those who aren't too keen on them and approach their resistance with compassion without compromising on the vision or giving in to pressure.

Here's another way to look at this. Leaders identify opportunities; managers identify obstacles. So, in a business meeting, Dr. Holmes excitedly tells of the new building—now, they'll be much more helpful to the community and much more influential on human lives!

Leaders take risks; managers avoid risks.

"But what about building permits?" Ezra Bird asks. "Have you thought of the property we're going to have to buy in this neighborhood? What happens if we can't make our budget next month? Remember, we barely paid our bills two months ago."

Leaders take risks; managers avoid risks.

As a leader, I've learned two things about this:
1) The larger risk is to refuse to take a risk. Nothing happens without taking risks.
2) If we wait until we're 100 percent sure, we're already too late.

As a wise person once said about baseball, "You can't steal second and still keep your foot on first."

For growth to happen, someone must take a risk. A leader pursues acquiring resources, but available resources limit managers. This means that if I am a leader and don't have the money, I can find some way to raise it. If I'm a manager, I'll say, "We do not have the money in the bank." Leaders see the empty coffers and know they can fill them; managers only see that the coffers are empty.

MAKING DECISIONS

I want to point out how most congregations make decisions. This is normally done in a board meeting, business meeting, session, or elders' meeting. The pastor has an excellent idea of how they can grow and increase their influence. He presents his ideas and then he pauses and asks the treasurer or financial secretary, "Do we have the money?"

I've learned that treasurers have been trained to move their heads only one way, and that is to say no. The leader is given the choice to act one of two ways following the treasurer's response. Unfortunately, visionaries often respond poorly to this all-too-frequent scenario—they allow the nearsighted to make decisions about the future. They throw veto power into the hands of the status quo before the idea has been fully discussed.

That's usually the death knell of moving ahead. Leaders, remember:
    1) The larger risk is to refuse to take a risk.
    2) If we wait until we're 100 percent sure, we're already too late.

By contrast, shortly after I became president of Beulah Heights Bible College, I saw this working flawlessly. I began to make changes in how we made decisions because the school was facing serious difficulties. We had an enrollment of eighty-seven students, the college was not accredited, and our staff was small, overworked, and underpaid.

> **Leaders see the empty coffers and know they can fill them; managers only see that the coffers are empty.**

We had to take some risks. We had to think differently. I proposed a simple rule. We have four questions we need to ask before we make our decisions, and they must be asked in the right order. As president, I could enforce this—and I did.

1) *Does this go along with our vision, mission, and core values?*

Another way to ask is this: Is it something we are supposed to do? Not every Bible college, church, or organization is supposed to do everything. In fact, the fewer things an organization does, the better off they are because they can focus and do all of them well.

For example, is a ministry to the homeless a vibrant and vital opportunity for God's church to express compassion? Yes, it is.

Is it part of our church's ministry? Maybe not.

Is reaching out to the refugees from Somalia a good thing to do? Absolutely, but it may not be part of the ministry that God has given us.

Are after-school tutoring and GED completion good things for a church to be involved in? Yes, but such educational programs may not be for us.

We can, however, resource those for whom it is their passion and challenge.

What we as a church, a Bible school, a para-church group must do is answer this question: Is this going to be part of our vision and mission? Does it flow with our core values? Are we considering this only because it's a good program that has been successful somewhere else?

   2) *Do we have the heart to make this happen?*
After all the discussion ends, it's going to take the right heart—the zeal, the commitment—to make anything happen. Another way to put it for the business community is: Do we have the organizational capacity to make this a reality?

3) *How will God be glorified?*
Notice I said *how* and not *if*. Many opportunities come our way that glorify God. We're Christians, and we sense needs or perceive opportunities. So, a better question is, *how* will this opportunity glorify God? We answer the question by saying, "Here are three ways we will glorify God if we expand our curriculum."

4) *How much will it cost?*
We don't discuss money until we've answered the first three questions. It's futile to consider the cost until we have positive answers to the first three.

Part of the rule we adopted was to *not* ask, "Do we have the money?" If we have answered the first three questions and still believe this is for us, then we move ahead. Part of that moving ahead is figuring out what it will cost. I've reminded the staff several times, "Salvation is free, but ministry is expensive." Once we know all those answers, we can begin to ask God to show us how to raise the money to do the ministry.

In many churches, and certainly at Beulah Heights, if our first question was whether we had the money, our doors probably would have been closed by now. As of 2003, we are the fastest-growing, predominately African-American Bible College in America. I believe it's because we're asking the correct questions and in the right order.

Here's another difference: Leaders are willing to say, "Let's acquire resources." Managers stop the discussion with, "But we don't have the resources."

Here are other differences: Leaders are people-centered, and managers are system-centered. Managers need to have policies and procedures manuals. Leaders hate policies and procedures manuals; managers love them. That is why we attend a church conference, and the managers quote the bylaws better than they do the Bible. They like systems. In fact, managers feel that if they can look at an organizational chart and move boxes across from one spot to another, they can transform the organization, but without a leader who will challenge and push past maximizing daily operations, we can move boxes all day long without effective results. Organizational charts don't contribute to the success of the corporation; people do. However, they *do* keep the organization's foundation strong so that the leader can dream, build, and expand.

Here's yet another way to see this: Leaders are idea-centered, and managers are plan-centered. That's a big difference because leaders say, "Here's what I'd like to do." Managers answer, "I need a plan before I can do this."

That is where fighting the battles between the two becomes inevitable. If they come out successful, it is because smart managers have taken the leader's good ideas and said, "Okay, here's the plan on how we can bring this about."

The best ladder-holders are excellent managers. Once they push past the discomfort of change and devise a plan, they can make things happen.

> **For leaders, people's approval is a want; for managers, approval is a need.**

Leaders can talk leadership language and manager language. Managers can talk only manager language. That makes it incumbent on leaders to build a bridge, walk across it, and shake hands with managers.

Finally, for leaders, people's approval is a want; for managers, approval is a need.

If I were speaking to a group, I'd say at this point, "As a leader, I want you to approve of me." Those who say they don't care what people think are lying. In fact, people who go around saying, "I don't care what people say," probably care the most, or they wouldn't think about others' opinions. As a leader, however, I also know that I don't need someone's good opinion to function.

When I speak at a conference or a banquet, I want to do a good job and want people to like what I say and agree with my message. But it's still only a want.

In almost any situation when I propose growth plans, not everyone will like my message. In fact, a few people might strongly disagree. If people disagree or disapprove, that will concern me. I might think about it quite a bit. I might pray that the situation would change. Regardless, the disapproval of others wouldn't stop me from moving forward with my ideas or speaking to another group tomorrow on the same topic. Yes, I want approval, but I don't need it.

Managers need approval, specifically from their leaders. That puts a burden on leaders to understand and keep managers' tanks filled. They can do that by simple affirmations. They can send e-mails, throw them a few "well dones," or mail a thank you note. They can poke their heads into a manager's office and say, "The choir did great yesterday. Thanks for your hard work." Managers constantly need to be appreciated, valued, and affirmed.

When I was a pastor, I had to be a self-motivator and a self-starter. In fact, I had to start despite the odds that were strongly against me, and that involved getting my tank filled in other ways than seeking others' affirmation. The manager can only start if somebody else fills the tank.

Ideas, concepts, visions, dreams, and entrepreneurship fill a leader's tank, put a smile on their faces, and excite them. Conversely, fulfillment, affirmation, and encouragement are the major motivators for managers. They are always working for somebody else, and they still need to feel significant because significance never goes away.

> Ideas, concepts, visions, dreams, and entrepreneurship fill a leader's tank, put a smile on their faces, and excite them. Conversely, fulfillment, affirmation, and encouragement are the major motivators for managers.

I'm the president of Beulah Heights Bible College, and everybody else on staff is my ladder holder. I get my tank filled all over the country. People don't usually call my dean and tell him what an outstanding job the college is doing. They say, "You're doing a great job" directly to me. They don't call my director of finance and say, "You ended in the black; you're doing great; you balanced the budget well." I hear those words personally.

Here's the point: leaders are responsible for filling managers' tanks, but managers don't fill leaders' tanks. In fact, leaders get into problems when they expect others to fill their tanks.

Haven't we all heard, "It's lonely at the top"?

> Managers get the most out of themselves, but leaders get the most out of others.

We've heard those words, but I don't believe them. It's not lonely at the top. If those at the top are lonely, it's because they didn't take anybody up there with them. It doesn't have to be lonely because there are other ladders there right next to them. Those at the top of their ladders are doing what makes them happy. They can enjoy each other. Simply put—a lonely leader doesn't fully understand the nature of leadership—it's not that there is *less* joy in leadership; the sources are just different.

Finally, managers get the most out of themselves, but leaders get the most out of others. Leaders, by their nature, constantly lead and, at the same time, inspire others. They're the cheerleaders and encouragers and enable others to say, "Yes! Yes! I can do that!"

In *Catalyst* magazine for April 2003, Ben Dyer wrote an editorial that starts with these words: "If it weren't for the people involved, this would be an easy business."[5] Then he quotes John Imlay, a now-prominent investor who led the software company Mandrin Sciences of America. Imlay said, "People are the key."[6]

That's what this book is about. People as the key.

The new prospective owner of the Atlanta Thrashers and Atlanta Hawks, David McDavid, gave an interview for the *Atlanta Journal Constitution* on May 2, 2003, that became a headline article for the sport's section.

He spoke about growing up around horses and added, "And that's not unlike sports teams, by the way. You've got to have the personnel if you want to win." In the same article, McDavid said, "But as an owner . . . I think my job would be to find the best general manager available . . . If I [were] going to try to make those decisions myself, I wouldn't need a general manager. But the fact is, I'm not competent to do that."[7]

A man of that caliber realized that his first job was to hire the best general manager and not try to do it himself.

6

CAN WE TURN LADDER HOLDERS INTO LADDER CLIMBERS?

"Where did you start your climb upward?" That's the question I'd like to ask every church and business leader. I'd like to know if they spotted a ladder, raced to it, and climbed to the top. Did they wait until someone waved them over and said, "Up you go"?

As I look at my own experience and consider the upward path of others, I suspect that most of them started at the bottom. That is, their careers began after they learned to hold the ladder securely for someone else to move smoothly upward.

They did more than hold the ladder. They observed, they learned, they saw the techniques used, and they understood where the ascending person was going. The day came when those same people who held ladders started their own climb upward.

That's not the end of the story either—at least not for the kind of leaders God calls into prominence in the church today. It's not enough for me to be at the top of the Beulah Heights Bible College ladder. I have another responsibility. God wants me to teach and empower others so they can move from the role of supporters to climbers. Wouldn't it be a shame if we left ladder holders be ladder holders forever?

The only time you start at the top is when you're digging a hole.

God has blessed me with leadership ability. If I had stayed at the bottom and held everybody's ladder, would that have been the best use of my divinely given talents?

Of course not.

Those of us in leadership positions remember—or I hope we do—where we started. At one time, I was the janitor, breakfast cook, and dishwasher at Beulah Heights. I held ladders so that others could succeed and minister.

Every effective business leader and every senior pastor started somewhere. They may have already had the gifts that eventually pushed them up the ladder, but most of them didn't start there. God's plan was already in place, but it started in a lowly position.

This is the biblical way. We read about Elisha, a man about whom the Bible records twice as many miracles as that of his mentor Elijah. But where did Elisha start? He held the ladder of the great prophet of Israel and faithfully followed until his turn came.

Jesus called twelve disciples. He planned great ministries for each of them. From the beginning, He knew that one day, He'd climb the ladder that would take Him all the way to heaven. He didn't leave the ladder empty but chose those with potential to become expert ladder climbers.

> At one time I was the janitor, breakfast cook, and dishwasher at Beulah Heights. I held ladders so that others could succeed and minister.

We're here today because Jesus saved us, of course. But we're also here today because His disciples started as supporters of Jesus until their times came to move upward. They are the ones who continued the work after Jesus ascended.

For example, I was born in India. Part of the reason I am in the United States today and involved in ministry is because of the faithfulness of one of the twelve—the apostle Thomas. As part of his ministry of going into all the world, he carried the gospel to my country and faithfully chose others to hold his ladder until his time came to leave this life. Thomas led others who then passed on the message through the centuries. I'm one of the modern beneficiaries of Thomas's faithfulness.

All of this is to say that we need to plan so that we turn ladder holders into ladder climbers. Otherwise, this becomes a self-serving club. I recruit a person to hold my ladder and say, "Now you stay there. You're not worthy of following my steps." Isn't it better to say, "This is where you are today, but this is not where God wants you to stay"? I can even add, "One day, you'll climb your own ladder, and you'll recruit those to support you while they grasp the first lessons of moving upward."

The need to train seems obvious, but I want to point out three things we need to do to ensure that we reach out, grab others by the hand, and help them take the first steps.

STEPS FOR TURNING LADDER HOLDERS TO LADDER CLIMBERS

The first step is what I call the *spiritual formation of a leader*. In this spiritual formation, we deal with security issues, finding purpose, and our destiny. At the age of forty-four, I finally discovered who I was and what I was called to do. I discovered that my primary motivation is to help others succeed. In fact, I have that statement written on the home page of my website (www.samchand.com or www.dream-releaser.org). It reads: "Samuel R. Chand Ministries, Inc. is an enhancing and collaborative process in developing leaders who in turn reproduce more leaders."

As I pondered that statement, I realized that I loved doing leadership development. It feeds my passion. It brought me fulfillment at a deeper level. As clearly as I perceived who I am, who I am not and what I don't want to do became just as clear. I am motivated by the opportunity to develop leaders.

As I've grappled with leadership development, it has occurred to me that we talk a lot about near-death experiences. I'm convinced that most people have what I call near-life experiences. They come close to being fully alive but never discover who they really are. They never work passionately at the things they're good at doing. Until we discover who we are, we won't climb the steps of the ladder that God wants us to climb.

We want to help people develop who they are. We want them to be able to answer these questions:
- » What am I passionate about?
- » What are my gifts and talents?
- » To what kind of work is God calling me?
- » What frustrates me?
- » What makes me cry?
- » What brings me joy?

If we can tune into those existential concepts, we'll get the best results and put people in the right places.

My second step is *skill formation.* I was greatly challenged when I read the book, *The Four Obsessions of an Extraordinary Executive* by Patrick Lencioni. Written as a parable, Lencioni tells the story about two companies that flourished. One of them grew and the people were happy and healthy. The second succeeded by cutting corners. Even though outwardly successful, the people in the second company were never as happy as those in the first. In the healthier-happier company, people knew who they were and what they were doing. They understood the soul of their company.[8]

That book so challenged me that I diligently worked to discover the soul of Beulah Heights Bible College. It took time and effort on my part, but I figured out the answer. In doing so, I also learned how to keep people aware of our five core values.

If anyone walks onto our campus today, they'll see posters of our values displayed—in every office, every classroom, every hallway, and even in every restroom. We have a five-color poster called "The Soul of Beulah Heights Bible College." On that poster, we list our vision, our mission, our core values, and our theme.

I'm not naïve enough to think that just putting up posters does the job. I just use them as constant reminders. I want to use whatever methods I can to promote the soul of Beulah Heights and to inculcate our values into our own souls. I do this based on a simple principle: *What we do must flow out of who we are.*

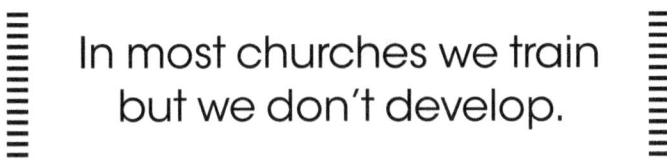

In most churches we train but we don't develop.

By contrast, in most churches we train but we don't develop.

Training carries a specific, narrow focus; developing is a broad focus.
  » Training is task-centered; development is people-centered.
  » Training is about a job as an usher, as a deacon, as a Sunday school teacher; development involves the whole person.

After we know who we are, *what* we do will always be a project. For example, in 2003 we had twenty-seven countries represented on our campus, so we promoted an International Day. We made it a big event. People wore their national regalia, presented their music, spoke their languages, and allowed us to sample their food.

When I addressed those present, I said, "Today is not an international day program. This is who we are."

I wanted to affirm them, celebrate our differences, and enable all of us to pull together. Two of our five core values are global missions and diversity. That is who we are. So, it's not a program; it's us. In churches, we often do not take people beyond tasks to really develop them spiritually, and that is why people come and people go, but they don't dig roots.

Rick Warren's book, *The Purpose-Driven Church*, helped me understand how this works. He uses the concept of baseball.

First base is salvation where *spiritual formation* begins. Here the focus is on spiritual discipline and developing us as individuals.

Second base would be what I call *skill formation*. This is where we change and begin to focus on others. We're trained to do ministry through our local church.

Third base is *strategic formation*. Here, we focus on extending God's kingdom on earth and leadership development. This refers to ministry to the church at large. We can be members of one church but have a heart for helping the homeless. Our church doesn't have a ministry to those needy people, but we remain members and involve ourselves in a para-church ministry to the homeless.[9]

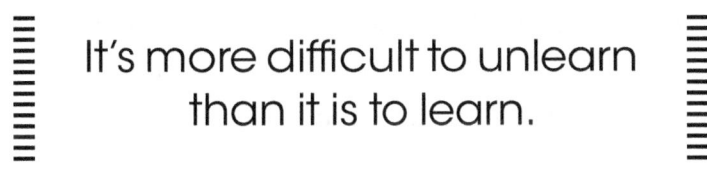

It's more difficult to unlearn than it is to learn.

That is what happens when we're not confined to ministry exclusively within the walls of our local building. We're developing our vision and focusing on global outreach.

To continue the baseball analogy, we can sometimes reach third base, but we don't win games by staying there. We have to make it to home plate. That is when we develop other leaders. For ladder climbers, bringing someone home is when we turn our ladder holders into our ladder climbers.

UNLEARNING AND LEARNING
In developing leadership skills, I've learned that it's more difficult to *unlearn* than it is to *learn*.

My experience with golf may help explain this. Years ago, when I lived in Oregon, a friend said, "Let's play golf."

"Yes, let's do that," I replied. I had never played golf before, but my friend was fairly good at the game. I enjoyed his company and figured there wasn't too much to learn.

A few days before we played, I stopped by a yard sale, bought an old set of clubs, and went out to the range. I felt highly confident because I had everything I needed. I put my baseball grip on my club and started hacking. Over a period of months, I became a pretty good hacker.

When I moved to Atlanta, friends invited me to play golf with them. I agreed to play but after a few games, I soon realized I was a hacker, and they were golfers.

One day a friend shook his head after I took six tries to get my ball about a hundred yards. "How do you hold your club?" he asked.

I showed him. I held my club like a baseball bat.

He showed me how I needed to change my grip by entwining my fingers. "Oh, that looks easy," I said.

Yes, it looked easy, but I couldn't get it. No matter how hard I tried to unlearn my old grip, I just couldn't get away from it. I had been holding my fingers that way for too long. It's been more than ten years since I tried to unlearn how to hold a golf club. I have never tried golf again. I just could not unlearn.

> The best use of power is to give it away. We give it away by investing in others.

The challenges I have encountered with unlearning didn't stop there. While I was a pastor in Michigan, I preached a sermon about obeying God's calling on our lives. Eleven people came forward for the altar call. Among them were our organist, pianist, bass guitarist, and drummer. Two weeks later, all of them left the church to enter Beulah Heights Bible College.

That left me without musicians. I decided I would learn to play the piano. I have a good ear, and I already had learned to play several songs in C, F, and G. Years earlier I had learned to play in what I called honky-tonk style. I got the job done as church musician, but I wasn't good, and I didn't know how to become a "real" musician.

Even today I still play honky-tonk style and can play almost any song people want to sing; I've learned a few techniques since then, but my style is still country style with a lot of chords. If a good music teacher tried to show me how to do runs (and they have tried), how to use the entire keyboard, or to expand my reach, I'd have to unlearn my fingering pattern to do that. I've been playing country style too long to unlearn.

Church leaders can save themselves a lot of heartache if they think carefully about and remain sensitive to those who join them after having been long-time members of another congregation. It's a big challenge for them to unlearn the way things were done in their previous church and to learn how it's done in the new. If leaders come pre-loaded with that knowledge, they can proactively assist new members in unlearning old methods and practices before it's too late.

I wonder what it would be like if I visited Joyful Praise Church next Sunday.

> Most of the leaders of my generation—the boomer generation—are **accidental leaders.** We stumbled into leadership.

Let's say I came inside, listened to a powerful message, the Holy Spirit convicted me of sin, and I raised my hand when the pastor extended an invitation for salvation. I walked down the aisle, and someone led me to a backroom, prayed with me, and taught me how to surrender my life to the Lord.

"What happens next?" I asked.

"Joyful Praise has a new converts' class."

That's good, I think to myself. Or perhaps it's a new members' class. That's good. I spend four to ten weeks learning. That's also good.

"What happens after that?"

"Just swim with the sharks. Do your best to make it." No one would actually say those words, but that's the unspoken message I'd probably receive from a church leader who doesn't have intentions to develop me spiritually or perhaps doesn't know how.

So, what happens next?

Most church leaders don't know. That's not good. But, it *could* be good if leaders took it a step beyond understanding what it means to be saved. In this scenario, after being taken into the back room and debriefed on the first steps of faith, that person could say, "Sam, for the next few weeks, we're going to invest ourselves in your spiritual development."

I may not be clear about what that means yet, but I would at least see that this isn't any ordinary church. This is a church that wants to walk with me, step into my mess, and train me to become a trusted follower of Jesus. That's a church I can trust. That's a church where I can plant myself, grow, and have hope for the future. Teachers and guides will take me from first base to second (skill formation), and I'll stay there until I'm ready to move on to third base.

"We're going to move you into strategic formation (third base)," says the senior pastor months after my conversion. "Our purpose is not for you to be a good church member. Our purpose is that one day you'll be doing what I'm doing right now. Maybe you won't pastor a church, but you'll develop other leaders. We recognize your leadership gifts, and we want to help you develop them."

How many congregations operate like that? Not many.

I'm suggesting that we strive for a holistic system to turn ladder holders into ladder climbers. We need to empower them and permit them to climb upward. I've learned that the best use of power is to give it away. We give it away by investing in others. This isn't for everyone. Not everyone is a leader.

There will always be people who love holding ladders and who have no desire to ascend them. That's an acceptable choice.

Most of the leaders of my generation—the boomer generation—are *accidental leaders*. We stumbled into leadership.

CAN WE TURN LADDER HOLDERS INTO LADDER CLIMBERS?

I don't remember anybody ever saying to me, "Sam, I see some potential in you."

People sent me signals, but no one said, "I'd like to walk this journey with you. You don't have to call me a mentor. Here's my phone number. Call me any time. In fact, if you don't mind, may I keep tabs on you and watch how you're doing?"

I wish someone had done that, and so do many other accidental leaders. I've proven this many times in conferences and meetings. "How many of you had somebody who intentionally developed you? Someone who took you under his or her wing?" In early 2003, I asked a group of 300 pastors in Cincinnati.

One man raised his hand. *Just one.*

Here's the challenge. We can only give what we have. We can't pass on what we don't possess because most of us teach the way we were taught. Are we going to inflict the same accidental leadership on the next generation? Or are we going to have a plan?

The new generation that's already filing into our churches wants to know where we're going. In the past, we may have been happy to go to church Sunday morning, midweek service, and enroll in the choir. Not so with this generation. They want to know if there is more.

> We need to get the right people on the bus and get the wrong people off. Then we need to get the right people in the right seats on the bus.

This is just as true in the business world. Those same people join the organization at the entry-level, but most of them don't want to stay there. If they're eagles, they want to fly. If they're ladder climbers, they don't want to stay on the ground.

As soon as they hit the ceiling—at whatever level—and realize the ladder they're on won't go any higher, they'll leave. They'll go to corporations with higher ceilings.

Jim Collins's bestseller *Good to Great* helped me understand this. He used the idea of getting the right people on the bus and getting the wrong people off. Then we need to get the right people in the right seats on the bus.[10]

The first two steps are pretty obvious—getting good people on the bus and getting rid of those who don't belong. The third step gives us heartache because once people get on the bus, we're not always sure what to do with them.

Collins's concept made me aware of one of the most excruciating years of my life. At Beulah Heights, I recognized that a person who had held my twenty-foot ladder did an excellent job—as long as I used that same ladder. When I decided to climb a forty-foot ladder, he couldn't hold it for me. The person who does an excellent job of holding a twenty-foot ladder may not be the same person we need if we want to go higher. It caused me intense pain to realize that just because someone is a committed, hard-working person of integrity doesn't mean we need them to help us move on to the next level. In other words, some ladder holders might be right for a season, but then you'll have to reassess as your goals and ambitions change.

How do we respectfully disengage them from our organization, and how do we respectfully bring in or promote from within someone who was holding a six-foot ladder and put that person in charge of forty-foot ladder holders? That means bypassing the twenty-foot holders or moving them out of their positions. That's never easy.

> "If he were a nonbeliever or a pagan, you could fire him, and he'd still be your friend."

I remember having a conversation with one of my mentors in the business community. I asked, "Have you ever fired a friend?"

"Yes."

"Can you help me put together a plan in which I can fire this friend and still keep him as my friend?"

He smiled and asked, "Is he a Christian?" "Absolutely. He's a dedicated, committed Christian."

"You can't do it then. If he were a nonbeliever or a pagan, you could fire him, and he'd still be your friend."

I stared at him and wondered how that could be. As I pondered his answer, I knew he was right. In the church, that's the challenge of leadership and a painful thing to realize.

Let's say I'm the pastor of a church with one hundred members. Marian is my secretary and she's a dedicated worker and has been in that position since 1980. She can type fast, and back in the 1980s and early 1990s, she spent many hours fighting with an inky mimeograph machine to put out a church bulletin every week. No matter what the task, all of us could depend on Marian. Many nights she stayed until long after dark and came in on Saturdays. No task was too big or too small for Marian.

We entered into a new century, and the church now has a thousand members. Marian was a wonderful, faithful, dependable ladder holder then. She isn't today.

She can't figure out the computer. She uses it, of course, but she hates it. She can't understand why we don't keep using the mimeograph because it's cheaper than running off bulletins on the laser printer. Spreadsheets confuse her, and only reluctantly does she use e-mail to communicate with members.

What happens now? Do we spare Marian's feelings and work around her? Do we fire her? Demote her by asking her to become the receptionist and answer the telephone? She was absolutely the best ladder holder when our ladder only reached twelve feet, but she can't handle one that rises to fifty feet. Should we keep seeking another twelve-foot ladder so we can make Marian happy?

Most growing organizations don't have another twelve-foot ladder, so people like Marian have maxed out. In a corporation, because we know they have hit their ceiling, we don't want to transfer a maxed-out worker from one department to the other. Such workers have chosen to remain at their current level and refuse to learn new skills to move ahead.

In a corporation, the secretary would know there's a forty-foot ladder coming up. She could preserve her job by learning the skills needed for the larger task. But what if she refuses? What if she chooses to retain the skill level she has right now? What if she agrees to develop her skills only under compulsion and obligation?

By contrast, let's say Hulda is the technology person and has spent a lot of time learning our information system. She understands and can program our software. She can run everything and catch all the bugs in the new systems. Our company now begins to expand because we're making more sales. We have more salespeople out there. Customers are buying from us off the web. Hulda has proven herself invaluable to the corporation, and she'll move ahead.

What about people like Marian who refuse to progress? They have chosen to become obsolete. That may sound harsh, but it's true.

This presents a great dilemma in leadership and is one of the most difficult tasks. As the leader, I have to address and respond to Marian's limitations. Even though I admire her and value her years of service, I must also admit that she is holding up the church's progress. Eventually, I will have to fire her. Thirty-year-old Hulda has been with the company only two years, but she will replace the fifty-three-year-old who has been a long-time employee but has stayed at the same skill level for the past twenty years.

In a business, people understand that their skills have not kept up with the demands. They may resent being fired, but they understand. But the church, however, faces a unique challenge. "I love the Lord. I work harder than anyone else," they wail. "No one is more committed to service than I am."

No matter how much I reason with her, Marian probably won't face the reality that she isn't able to work with anything more than a twelve-foot ladder. She can't understand why we no longer need short ladders.

We need different ladder holders for different levels in the organization. Old leaders are rarely new leaders because people continue to view the organization at the level they came to it, whereas new leaders see it as it is now.

For example, a church leader who joined the church when it had one hundred members will have a difficult time leading the church when it is 1,000 members because he still thinks of the church as it "used to be."

So, what do we do?

7
ARE WE LOOKING UP THE LADDER?

Several times, I have wrestled with how to handle people who refuse to grow with the organization. One of the most helpful things I did was to consult other leaders. How did they handle such situations?

A quote from Ken Blanchard helped me immensely. He came into prominence in the late 1970s when he co-wrote *The One Minute Manager*. In a written interview by Patricia Baldwin in *Private Clubs*, Blanchard said:

> *We're only as good as the person who's answering the phone, the person who's greeting the customers, the person who deals with complaints. Nobody cares who's the president of a company.*

He goes on to say, "If you create a great human organization, then everything else takes care of itself."[11]

In the previous chapter, I mentioned that Patrick Lencioni's book *The Four Obsessions of an Extraordinary Executive*[12] profoundly affected me. He started talking about the soul of the organization. I had signs called "The Soul of Beulah Heights Bible College" plastered all over the walls, but I knew that, by themselves, they wouldn't make any difference. I had to spend time with the ladder holders and help them see the significance of their roles; that way, the signs would mean something—they would express *their* attitudes and values—not just mine. Because I spent time nurturing the significance of their roles, the signs only reinforced what they had already come to believe.

> **If you create a great human organization, then everything else takes care of itself.**

In the first chapter of this book, I pointed out that developing leaders takes time. After I thought about this a great deal, I asked my assistant to set up half-hour appointments between me and everyone on staff—full-time and part-time. When I met with them, I explained that this was not a job evaluation; their jobs may change, but nobody would be dismissed.

I reviewed their job description and what they were doing for the college. I then allowed them to tell me about their job.

"What is your passion?" I asked. "Where do you find your greatest joy?"

One person said, "I hate what I'm doing." "What would you love to do instead?"

She told me, and we made changes. She is now doing the job she loves. Later, she said, "Now I look forward to coming to work every day."

They were all good people, and, to use Jim Collins's metaphor, they all belonged on the bus—we just didn't have everyone in the right seat. It was my fault as president that they didn't feel fulfilled or didn't like the ladder they had to hold. Out of those conversations, I made three changes by shifting personnel. At that time, I terminated no one.

I tell my receptionists, "You are the director of first impressions."

The principle is simple. If people are joyful and love what they're doing, it will show in everything they do. When they answer the phone, the caller will know they're happy in their jobs.

I tell my receptionists, "You are the director of first impressions." I know that before people meet the president, go into any of the classrooms, or listen to any of our great instructors, they will hear a voice on the telephone. They'll see that person as soon as they open the office door.

We also needed to have curb appeal on our campus. There's no litter on our grounds. No one will see paper cups on the ground or candy wrappers blowing in the wind. We want visitors to see a caring, efficient organization no matter where they look, but that is only accomplished when a person's position aligns with their strengths and passions.

> You have to know what you do best and do it. The notion that you can make it at anything you want to do just isn't true.

Expert Bernie Marcus, the co-founder and former CEO of The Home Depot, puts it this way:

> *You have to know what you do best and do it. The notion that you can make it at anything you want to do just isn't true. There are things you can and*

can't be successful at. You have to sit down and measure your skills—strong and weak—and then build toward the strengths.

The author of the article points out that Marcus learned to focus after he had previously failed with another company. He built a home improvement colossus. "My strengths were as an entrepreneur and a merchant but not on the day-to-day. So I focused on those areas, as well as on people, and *surrounded myself with great operators.*"

He was talking about ladder holders. He goes on to say, "You are only as good as the people around you. So surround yourself with good people"[13]

Paraphrasing his words, we can only go as high as the person holding the ladder lets us. Our height is controlled not by us but by the people on the ground level.

The president and chief operating officer of the Ritz-Carlton Hotel, Simon Cooper, said in an interview:

My challenge is how to continue the company's growth, based upon our founding principles. Therefore, I'm focused on both human and financial capital. After all, we're not going to be successful if we don't attract and retain the absolute best human capital as well as financial capital.[14]

Anyone who's ever stayed at a Ritz-Carlton knows the difference is not necessarily the rooms. We can get good rooms at other hotels as well. The difference is their service. They profile customers, know what they prefer, and provide for their comfort.

S. Truett Cathy, founder of Chick-fil-A, the fastest-growing fast-food franchise in the world, gives his recipe for business success:
> *It requires a lot of time and effort to make sure you have the right people working the right jobs, but we believe it is time well spent.*[15]

In other words—the payoff is customer satisfaction.

Another article written in the *Atlanta Journal Constitution* said that people skills are most important. They prefer attitude to aptitude. "Given a choice, Georgia employers say they'd take an adaptable 'people' person over a technically proficient worker."[16] This conclusion came from a survey conducted by the Metro Atlanta Chamber of Commerce in early 2003.

The first question to Leonard Roberts, president of Radio Shack, in an interview that appeared in Delta's Sky magazine, was: "What is the greatest challenge your industry faces?"

Roberts is in a technical field, and I would have assumed he would refer to handling technical challenges or keeping up with the rapid growth in electronic breakthroughs. Here was his answer:

> Our biggest challenge is making sure we have the right people on board, trained properly, and qualified to provide the answers Americans need about technology.

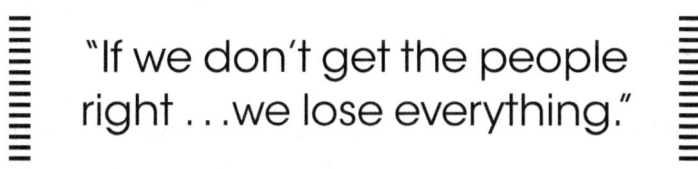

"If we don't get the people right...we lose everything."

There it was again: people before technology.

Here is the last question and answer of that interview:

"What if it [strategy] goes wrong?"

"If we don't get the people right, it all goes away. We lose everything."[17]

Wayne Gretzky, who is recognized as the greatest ice hockey player in history, was asked, "What's the most important thing you've learned as a restaurateur?"

> That your partner's gotta know what he's doing. I have a great partner. He's been in the restaurant

business with his family for more than 50 years. They know what they're doing. The best thing you can do is make sure you pick the right people, and I've got a great partner. (Emphasis mine)[18]

In an interview with Gerd H. Klauss, president and CEO of Volkswagen of America, the interviewer asked:
The head of every major automobile company claims that his company is the best, but Volkswagen truly is a global trademark. What is it that makes the company so successful?

As part of his answer, Klauss said, "Volkswagen attracts people who are proud to be different, who don't always follow the mainstream."[19]

To put Klauss' sentiment into my language, there are certain people we want to attract as ladder-holders.

8
HOW DID JESUS CHOOSE LADDER HOLDERS?

"**H**ow did Jesus choose ladder holders?" I asked myself that question several times, and I think Luke 5:1-11 holds the answer. In that account, Luke records the incident where Peter, James, and John fished all night and caught nothing. After they had given up and were busily washing their nets, Jesus boarded one of the boats, taught the people, and then told Peter to go out and fish again. Even though they who were professional fishermen had caught nothing, Peter did what Jesus told him. To his amazement, they caught so many fish their nets broke, and they had to ask other fishermen to help them.

The account ends when Jesus tells them that from now on, they won't be catching fish. They'll be catching people. This story marks the beginning of Jesus's ministry—calling the first three of what would eventually be His twelve disciples.

Although I had read the passage many times, one day I noticed that Luke 5:10 (AMP) refers to "James and John, the sons of Zebedee, who were partners with Simon [Peter]."

This means they were partners before Jesus called them. Jesus didn't break up their partnership. If we follow the life of Jesus, we see that He had just called His three major ladder holders. After that, everywhere He went, He always took that trio with Him *as a group*. If they were partners in the fishing business, given the culture and the norms of that time, it is fair to assume that their fathers and perhaps grandfathers had been partners.

> Peter, James, and John were partners before Jesus called them.
>
> Jesus didn't break up their partnership.

Here's how Jesus operated with the three partners. One day, He went to the house of Jairus. The man's daughter had died, and Jesus took the threesome with him. They were with Him at the Mount of Transfiguration. At the end of His journey, when He prayed at Gethsemane, Jesus called all His disciples and then took the three men farther into the garden with Him.

This is the way the Lord worked. He first called a group of twelve. But even there, He chose individuals. In Luke

5:27-28, Luke records, "And after these things he went forth, and saw a publican, named Levi, sitting at the receipt of custom: and he said unto him, Follow me. And he left all, rose up, and followed him."

The word translated as "saw" in this passage is the Greek word *theaomai*. Although there are a dozen words in Greek for seeing, this word rarely appears. It carries the idea of seeing attentively—staring—and is sometimes translated as "to behold." Scholars call it a solemn word that "is used for visionary seeing and the apprehension of higher realities."[20]

Although not a common word in the New Testament, *theaomai* has four distinct meanings. Each one stresses the action of the person who is seeing.
1) To observe with desire
2) To observe for a time
3) To spend time with
4) To look or study closely

Pay special attention to the fourth meaning. That's the point Luke made when he used *theaomai*. Jesus wasn't looking around casually. He scrutinized and focused carefully. It is as if Jesus gazed thoroughly into the man, and then, and only then, did he say, "Follow me."

Jesus recruited Levi with a purpose in mind. All through the Gospels, Matthew is just one of the twelve, but Jesus had a special purpose for him. Levi, also known as Matthew, was someone who knew how to keep accurate records—that was his business as a tax collector. What the former tax collector didn't realize was that, even then, Jesus was preparing him to write an accurate account of events. It would be called the Gospel according to Matthew, the first book in the New Testament.

> **People are recruited as ladder holders as a group, but they continue as individuals.**

Jesus is still doing the same kind of *theaomai* today. He is gazing at us on two levels—our role as part of the group and as individuals.

Here's the point: people are recruited as ladder holders as a group, but they continue as individuals. At Beulah Heights Bible College, when I was dealing with personnel issues, people repeatedly asked each other three questions. (Of course, none of them asked me.)

    1) Does Sam see what we see? Everyone in our office knew the weak links. They could see the incompetence. They didn't think of those individuals as bad

people, but only as those who were unable to get the job done.
2) If Sam sees what we see, why doesn't he do something about it?
3) If Sam doesn't see what we see, what kind of leader is he?

Eventually, I asked some people to leave the bus, invited new ones inside, and changed the seating arrangements. As a result, we began to function more efficiently. That's when I learned about the three questions they had been asking each other.

After I made the changes, the people came to me with statements that started with one word: finally.

"Finally, somebody did something."

"Finally, somebody saw what we've known all along."

"Finally, somebody had the courage to make it happen."

Until then, I didn't realize that they were questioning my leadership—and they were right to do so—because they saw the entire organization suffering from what they considered my inaction.

I did the right things; I just did some of them a little late.

9

WHOSE LADDER ARE YOU HOLDING?

In reading what I've written so far, some may assume that if we're leaders, all we need to do is concentrate on and develop other ladder-holders. That's only half of the assignment.

Here's the other half: Every true disciple of Jesus Christ holds somebody's ladder. That's God's plan. We need each other, and we fulfill God's plan when we hold others' ladders.

> God has called all of us to hold ladders for others.

We tend to forget that those of us who are leaders are ladder climbers and also ladder holders. Furthermore, we'll always be ladder-holders even if we're high-stepping climbers. Effective leaders understand that they are holding someone's ladder, whether it's the business partner's ladder, that of another church pastor, or a denominational leader. God has called all of us to hold ladders for others.

Effective leaders recognize two facts:
   1) In leadership, we will always need ladder holders.
   2) In leadership, we will also hold someone else's ladder. We are meant to support, assist, and help others in their climb upward.

Another way to get to this is to ask ourselves: What kind of ladder holder would I like? For example, earlier in this book, I wrote about needing ladder holders with five characteristics. They must be strong, attentive, faithful, firm, and loyal. Isn't it obvious that we need to be the kind of people we want others to become? If we want to develop superior ladder holders, we need to become superior ladder holders ourselves.

If you are a leader, here's my challenge to you: Whose ladder can you hold? What business leader can you mentor? Instead of looking at potential recruits and asking, "How can they serve me?" ask, "How can I serve them?"

God always intended for service to be a street where we travel both ways. It is the law of reciprocity, and it teaches us that what we give will come back to us. That's absolutely true; however, the problem is that we can only give what we have. We can only pass on what we possess. If we aren't good ladder holders, how can we expect to have good ladder holders helping us?

It makes me think of the law of tithing in the Old Testament. God required all faithful Jews to give 10 percent of their income to support the priests (hold their ladders). That's not the end of the law. The priests then gave ten percent to support the high priest. Even the priests had ladders to hold. That's always God's way of working.

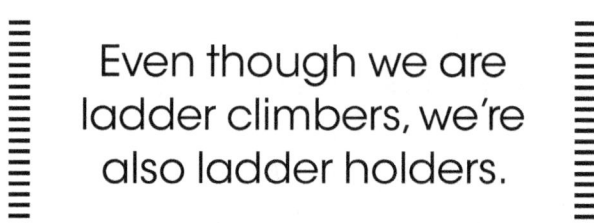

Even though we are ladder climbers, we're also ladder holders.

If each of us is able to acknowledge the principle, it means that although we're leaders, we're also ladder holders. Here are a few more questions for us to ponder:

» Do I possess those five essential qualities of good ladder holders?
» Do I intentionally hold someone else's ladder?
» Am I a dependable ladder holder?
» When was the last time I walked past a visionary leader and said, "I really like his vision and like where he's going. I want to work alongside him and assist him by holding his ladder"?

> » When was the last time I asked, "What leader can I help?" (Too often we are only looking for people to help us.)
> » What does it say about us if we always seek someone to hold our ladder, but we're unwilling to hold another person's ladder?

There's an old saying that most preachers will travel to the other corner of the world to preach a sermon, but they won't cross the street to hear one. Is that true of me? Here are other questions to ask ourselves:

> » When was the last time I attended a leadership conference when I wasn't a speaker?
> » When did I go to a conference just to hear somebody else?
> » When was the last time I read a book and thought, I really like this, and then corresponded with the author?
> » When was the last time I saw somebody else's advertisement in a magazine and said, "I want to serve that person"?

It's the principle, which is also in the Bible, that we reap what we sow. If we sow holding ladders, we reap those who will hold our ladders. We receive by giving. This is just as true with ladder holding as anything else.

It's not easy for many of us in leadership to be ladder holders, especially those of us, like me, who are accidental leaders. Accidental leaders may have a more difficult time tracing their path to impart lessons learned along the way to others traveling a similar path. While their travels began a long time ago, their framework for effective leadership comes into focus the moment they realize they are established leaders. And, in my case, I never had my own ladder holders during those formative years.

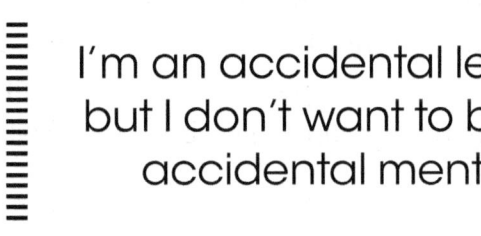

I'm an accidental leader, but I don't want to be an accidental mentor.

I still remember the question my friend, Tom Fortson, asked me. Tom, the executive vice president of Promise Keepers, visited Beulah Heights one day and I gave him a tour around the college. On the steps to our chapel, he paused and asked, "Can you tell me when you became a leader?"

"No, I really can't," I said. Immediately my mind flashed back to something John Maxwell once told me about himself. If Tom Fortson had asked John when he became a leader, John would have known how to answer. For him, that defining moment happened during his elementary school days. The class planned a mock courtroom. The students chose the jury, the defendant, the defense attorney, and the prosecutor. The class elected John the judge. Because of their confidence in his ability, on that day, John knew he was going to become a leader.

I told that story to Tom Fortson and added, "I haven't had that kind of epiphany in my life. I've just been one of those to whom leadership was slowly revealed."

Tom's question has stayed with me, and I've thought about it many times. When I speak in churches, I discover that most of the senior pastors are also accidental leaders. It's just as true when I ask about leadership in the marketplace.

I'm seventy-two years old at the time of writing this book. I can't recall a single instance during my time in Bible college, seminary, or denominational experience when anyone pointed out my leadership ability. Not once has a single person ever said to me, "I see potential in you. Good things are going to happen in your life. Could I walk with you? May I hold your ladder?" Fine individuals have given me excellent advice; others have opened doors for me. As I mentioned earlier, no one has walked with me as my ladder holder. The realization that no one openly and intentionally mentored me has caused me to become more intentional in mentoring others. That's my way of holding ladders.

> As leaders, when we start upward, our most **important** decision is to choose the right ladder holders; as ladder holders, our most important decision is to select which ladders we hold.

For some people, that ability flows freely, and they simply do it. Because the ability comes naturally, they rarely think much about it. Others like me don't find it easy because we have no role model to guide us. Because I was never intentionally mentored, I don't know the tracks to run on. I'm an accidental leader, but I don't want to be an accidental mentor.

Here are some large and final questions:
- » Whose ladder are you holding right now?
- » Who is climbing upward and trusting you to be there at the bottom, bracing the ladder for him or her?
- » Who is climbing high because you stepped out of the way and said, "Let me support you"?
- » Who will look back one day and say, "I rose forty-five feet in the air because you held my ladder"?

We have opportunities to be somebody's ladder holder. Because no one has done it for us, it may be difficult to intentionally commit ourselves to holding ladders, but it's not impossible. And it doesn't excuse us. It only means that it may take a little more effort for us accidental leaders to become intentional servants. But we can do it. We can commit ourselves to learning how to hold ladders so others can climb high, and some of them may even soar above us.

Nobody ever climbed Mt. Everest without a team. People climb Stone Mountain outside Atlanta because it's a relatively easy path and they don't need a team. No matter how high we go, we should be holding somebody else's ladder—that's God's plan.

> When we accomplish great things on our own ladder, we remember what we've done. When we intentionally hold others' ladders and they accomplish great things, they remember us. Their achievements become our legacy.

As leaders, when we start upward, our most important decision is to choose the right ladder holders; as ladder holders, our most important decision is to select which ladders we hold.

Here's one way I like to think of it. When we accomplish great things on our own ladder, we remember what we've done. When we intentionally hold others' ladders and they accomplish great things, they remember us. Their achievements become our legacy.

APPENDIX
TEACHING THIS MATERIAL

You may find an opportunity to teach this material. I hope you will. To facilitate that, I have placed an outline of the material in this book on the pages that follow. Please feel free to copy the outline with the blanks as a handout. After that is a completed outline. This book puts flesh on that skeleton.

WHO IS HOLDING YOUR LADDER?

In leadership, the most important decision you will make is **s**_____ your ladder holders.
   1) Is someone holding your L_____?
   2) What kind of P_____ is holding your ladder?
       » Do you have to constantly R_____ them?
       » Are they C_____ or intentional?
       » Do they have their eye on Y_____ or are they looking around?
       » Do they have a firm grip on your "ladder" or V_____?
   3) Qualities of an effective ladder holder:
       » S_____
       » A_____
       » F_____

WHO'S HOLDING YOUR LADDER?

> » F_____
> » L_____

4) Ladder holders must be T_____.
   > » Very few ministers have Q_____ and T_____ ladder holders.
   > » Your armor bearer/A_____ may not necessarily be your ladder holder.
   > » People need C_____ instruction.

5) Ladder P_____ and perspective
   > » The greatest tragedy is to climb to the top of the ladder, only to find your ladder is leaning against the W_____ building.
   > » Assess
   > » W_____ you want to go.
   > » W_____ you're on the ladder.
   > » W_____ tools you need up there—you can't keep going up and down.

6) Two basic categories of ladder holders
   > » L_____
   > » M_____

LEADERS

Conceptualize outcome by working from the **F**_____ back to the **P**_____

Embrace a **M**_____ perspective (big picture).

Favor **I**_____ thinking

R_____ flair

Emphasis on the **W**_____ and **W**_____

I_____ and motivating **E**_____ by change

Move **Q**_____
Identify **O**_____
Take **R**_____
Pursue acquisition of **R**_____
P_____-centered
I_____-centered
People's approval is a **W**_____.

MANAGERS
Conceptualize plans by working from the **P**_____ to the **P**_____
Embrace a **M**_____ perspective (snapshot)
Favor **R**_____ thinking
P_____ of the status quo
Emphasis on the **H**_____ and **W**_____
C_____ and **D**_____
T_____ by change
Move and decide **S**_____
Identify **O**_____
Avoid **R**_____
Actions limited by **A**_____ resources
S_____-centered
P_____-centered
People's approval is a **N**_____.

SUMMARY
Managers get the most out of **T**_____. Leaders get the most out of **O**_____.
 1) Turning ladder **H**_____ into ladder **C**_____

- » S_____ formation
- » Security issues
- » Finding purpose and destiny
- » S_____ formation
- » Helping other ladder-holders
- » Delegation
- » Communication
- » S_____ formation
- » Plan for developing other ladder-holders
- » Mentoring: See it (K_____), pursue it (G_____), and help others see it (S_____)
- » Empowering others

2) Whose ladder are Y_____ holding?
- » In leadership, you will always need L____ holders.
- » In leadership, you will always hold someone else's L_____.

Conclusion: In leadership, the most important decision you will make is selecting your ladder holders.

WHO IS HOLDING YOUR LADDER?

In leadership, the most important decision you will make is **selecting** your ladder holders.

1) Is someone holding your LADDER?
2) What kind of PERSON is holding your ladder?
- » Do you have to constantly REMIND them?
- » Are they CASUAL or intentional?
- » Do they have their eye on YOU or are they looking around?
- » Do they have a firm grip on your "ladder" or VISION?

3) Qualities of an effective ladder holder
    » STRONG
    » ATTENTIVE
    » FAITHFUL
    » FIRM
    » LOYAL
4) Ladder holders must be TRAINED.
    » Very few ministers have QUALIFIED and TRAINED ladder holders.
    » Your armor bearer/ASSISTANT may not necessarily be your ladder holder.
    » People need CLEAR instruction.
5) Ladder POSITION and perspective
    » The greatest tragedy is to climb to the top of the ladder, only to find your ladder is leaning against the WRONG building.
    » Assess
    » WHERE you want to go.
    » WHY you're on the ladder.
    » WHAT tools you need up there—you can't keep going up and down.
6) Two basic categories of ladder holders
    » LEADERS
    » MANAGERS

LEADERS

Conceptualize outcome by working from the **FUTURE** back to the **PRESENT**.
Embrace a **MACRO** perspective (big picture)

Favor **INNOVATIVE** thinking
REVOLUTIONARY flair
Emphasis on the **WHAT** and **WHY**
INSPIRING and motivating
EXCITED by change
Move **QUICKLY**
Identify **OPPORTUNITIES**
Take **RISKS**
Pursue acquisition of **RESOURCES**
PEOPLE-centered
IDEA-centered
People's approval is a **WANT**.

MANAGERS
Conceptualize plans by working from the **PAST** to the **PRESENT**.
Embrace a **MICRO** perspective (snapshot)
Favor **ROUTINE** thinking
PROTECTOR of the status quo
Emphasis on the **HOW** and **WHEN**
CONTROLLING and directing
THREATENED by change
Move **SLOWLY**
Identify **OBSTACLES**
Avoid **RISKS**
Actions limited by **AVAILABLE** resources
SYSTEM-centered
PLAN-centered
People's approval is a **NEED**.

SUMMARY

Managers get the most out of **THEMSELVES**. Leaders get the most out of **OTHERS**.

1) Turning ladder HOLDERS into ladder CLIMBERS
    » SPIRITUAL formation
    » Security issues
    » Finding purpose and destiny
    » SKILL formation
    » Helping other ladder-holders
    » Delegation
    » Communication
    » STRATEGIC formation
    » Plan for developing other ladder holders
    » Mentoring: See it (KNOW), pursue it (GROW), and help others see it (SHOW)
    » Empowering others

2) Whose ladder are YOU holding?
    » In leadership, you will always need LADDER-holders.
    » In leadership, you will always hold someone else's LADDER.

Conclusion: In leadership, the most important decision you will make is selecting your ladder holders.

ENDNOTES

1 *USA Today* ad by Randall Murphy, March 19, 2001. p. 2A.
2 Dr. Sam Chand and Cecil Murphy, *Futuring: Leading Your Church into Tomorrow* (Grand Rapids, MI: Baker Books, 2002).
3 Chand and Murphy, *Futuring*.
4 Chand and Murphy, *Futuring*, 8.
5 *Catalyst magazine*, article author Ben Dyer, April 2003. p. 8
6 Ibid, quoting John Imlay.
7 *Atlanta Journal Constitution*, David McDavid quote, May 2, 2003. p. A12.
8 Patrick Lencioni, *The Four Obsessions of an Extraordinary Executive: A Leadership Fable* (San Francisco, CA: Jossey-Bass, 2020).
9 Rick Warren, *The Purpose-Driven Church: Every Church Is Big in God's Eyes* (Grand Rapids, MI: Zondervan, 1995).
10 Jim Collins, *Good to Great: Why Some Companies Make the Leap . . . and Others Don't* (New York, NY: Harper Business, 2001).
11 Kenneth Blanchard and Spencer Johnson, *The One Minute Manager* (New York, NY: William Morrow & Co, 1982).
12 Lencioni, *The Four Obsessions of an Extraordinary Executive*.
13 Bernie Marcus quote in article, catalystmagazine.net, 1. p. 18.
14 Simon Cooper quote in an interview, *Leader*, vol 25, no 1, p. 126
15 S. Truett Cathy quote, *Atlanta Journal Constitution*, April 7, 2002, p. C1
16 *Atlanta Journal Constitution* article quote, January 5, 2003, p. C1
17 *Delta Sky Magazine* interview with Leonard Roberts, "Radio Shack's Leonard Roberts" por Lisa E. Davis, September 2000, p. 44
18 Wayne Gretzky quote, "Beyond Greatness" by Mark Seal, *Celebrated Living*, Winter 2002, p. 32
19 Gerd H. Klauss interview quote, *Leader*, Vol. 26, no 1, p. 41
20 Geoffrey W. Bromiley, *Theological Dictionary of the New Testament: Abridged in One Volume* (Williams B. Eerdemans Publishing, 1985), 707.

AVAIL +

TRY FOR 30 DAYS **AND RECEIVE**
**THE SEQUENCE TO SUCCESS
BUNDLE** FREE

$79 VALUE

+ BOOK
+ STUDY GUIDE
+ ONLINE COURSE
+ LIVE CLASS
+ MORE

The Art *of* Leadership

This isn't just another leadership collective...this is the next level of networking, resources, and empowerment designed specifically for leaders like you.

Whether you're an innovator in ministry, business, or your community, **AVAIL +** is designed to take you to your next level. Each one of us needs connection. Each one of us needs practical advice. Each one of us needs inspiration. **AVAIL +** is all about equipping you, so that you can turn around and equip those you lead.

THEARTOFLEADERSHIP.COM/CHAND

THE BIGGEST TSUNAMI
ABOUT TO HIT THE CHURCH IS
SUCCESSION

Approximately one-third of the churches in America will go through a pastoral transition in the next 10 years.

Get the outside help you need in one of the most delicate seasons of your ministry.

EXPERTS IN SUCCESSION AND TRANSITION PLANNING

EXPAND
CONSULTING PARTNERS

To set up a free consultation visit
EXPANDCONSULTINGPARTNERS.COM

PAY *WHATEVER* YOU CAN!

WE WILL LET YOU SET YOUR OWN TUITION PRICE.

TO DATE WE HAVE GIVEN AWAY $5 MILLION IN FINANCIAL AID

Amazing things happen when a group of like-minded, high-achieving and diverse leaders gather with one goal in mind: to succeed like never before. The Sam Chand Leadership Institute is a place where you can network, learn and be empowered to reach your potential and see success in your life's work.

Leadership is a journey, and you don't have to take it alone! If you're tired of the status quo and are ready to go to a whole new level, you're in the right place.

SAM CHAND
LEADERSHIP INSTITUTE

CHECK OUT OFFER AT
SAMCHANDLEADERSHIPOFFER.COM

www.ingramcontent.com/pod-product-compliance
Lightning Source LLC
Chambersburg PA
CBHW070542090426
42735CB00013B/3054